Secretary Albright,

Thank you for your service, but also your experiences, wisdom and warnings. My experiences are mostly from flying airplanes, but when I needed to emphasize the dangers of big Risk on the horizon I used your words about facism (page 204) to help the reader understand.

Ultimately I'd like to think safe landings points toward quality control for citizenship.

I have included a couple more copies for other in the Albright Stonebridge Group. If anyone would like to discuss these issues or can help me get these concepts into the public domain, I would appreciate it.

Fly Safe — Brad Bartholomew
9 Nov 2020

SAFE
LANDINGS

a Flight Plan and Checklist for Building a Renewed America

by Captain Brad Bartholomew

Print ISBN: 978-1-09833-026-2

eBook ISBN: 978-1-09833-027-9

"Either you deal with what is reality, or you can be sure reality is going to deal with you."

—ALEX HALEY, *ROOTS: THE SAGA OF AN AMERICAN FAMILY*

TABLE OF CONTENTS

Foreword:

THE BIG RISK DOCTRINE

"The most difficult thing is the decision to act, the rest is merely tenacity."

—AMELIA EARHART

Many months ago, we Americans scoffed at China for denying they were facing what I like to call Big Risk. At the time I rewrite this foreword on July 29, 2020, America continues to grapple with the exact same risk. However, I would argue that the biggest problem America faces currently is not the coronavirus, but the reality that we initially faced it—and continue to face it—as a divided nation thus delaying timely or coordinated responses.

COVID-19 is also highlighting another reality: when it comes to global Big Risk, we are all in it together. In the business of aviation, the entire industry must always maintain vigilance to keep Big Risk at bay, or at least carefully sidestep it. When Big Risk does suddenly erupt, however, it's the pilots who must deal with it. For the past forty years of my career as a pilot, I have flown planes for the United States

Air Force and commercial jets for a major U.S. airline. As a seasoned pilot, and one quite familiar with the idea of Big Risk, here are the three questions I use to determine when to take action when I sense trouble brewing on the horizon.

---

1. Can this risk annihilate me, or us?

2. Am I traveling toward the risk or away from it?

3. Am I getting too close to the Big Risk?

Let's say I'm flying a Boeing 737 with a hundred and fifty of my new best friends in the cabin, and I happen to look out the front window and see a line of thunderstorms gathering from a hundred miles away; big, black thunderheads and a bank of rolling, dark clouds.

If the optimum weather conditions exist, I can simply make a fifteen-degree turn upwind and smoothly fly past the risk without alerting anyone in the cabin as to what's going on, and without impacting my fuel log. But if I keep flying another fifty miles toward the risk *before* turning, I'll need to make a forty-five-degree course correction to sidestep that risk. At this point, my fuel log will be slightly impacted, but for the most part, I'll still be in control of my future. Because of the turning radius of flying through the sky at five hundred miles per hour, the last possible moment I can turn away from the enormous risk encompassing my front window is at about ten miles away from it, which will put me at risk for losing control of my fuel log. In this last scenario, and probably without meaning to, I have foolishly backed myself into a corner.

One of the undeniable truths about traveling toward Big Risk is that if you get too close, it can suddenly overwhelm you, just like the powerful undertow of ocean waves that can pull you under if you're not paying strict attention. However, once you are inside Big Risk, the game fundamentally changes.

It's now a game of survival.

And the rules of engagement in a survival situation are completely different than the daily routine of problem-solving basic tasks, or meeting challenges or goals. After all, there are hundreds of safe paths around thunderstorms. Pilots face these kinds of potentially severe weather conditions nearly every day in the air. Yet the biggest risk is not the storm itself, but that I, as Captain, will make some kind of fatal mental error. If my biases, my ego, or my pride lead me to believe, even just for a moment, that my superior flying skills and high-tech airplane are more powerful than Mother Nature herself, then everyone onboard may be in peril. Good pilots, *smart pilots*, understand that Mother Nature is always in charge. We can be great dance partners, but she leads. We must always follow.

From my years of dealing with stress and risk in the air, I've come to believe that the most important ingredient is not the quality of the first course correction I make around danger, it's *when I make* that first course correction. I have also learned that the first course correction I make in the air is probably the first of many, and to land safely every time, I will need to make as many course corrections as are necessary.

This is probably a good time to point out that denial doesn't work in the air. When we are flying an airplane, pilots understand implicitly that we must deal with reality—or it will deal with us.

If the answers to the first two questions above are yes, then question three becomes paramount: But on the ground, in a large group under stress, there will be some debate regarding the first two questions, but for the most part, we humans—no matter how badly we are divided—should be able to get a group consensus. Why do I say this? Well, it's pretty simple. Stress often pulls us apart. The palpable fear of Big Risk, however, can help bring us back together.

Unfortunately, for a variety of reasons from my experiences of observing groups of people traveling toward risk, do not expect the group to ever reach a consensus while answering question three. Each one of us, under stress, will have a slightly different feeling, opinion, or answer to the third question: Are we getting too close to the Big Risk?

Remember when I said the coronavirus was not our biggest threat, it was facing the virus as a divided nation? America unfortunately never collectively asked ourselves the first two easy questions. Naturally, by the time we got deeply concerned, we stumbled badly over the third question: Are we too close?

The wisdom, and the powerful trigger of the Big Risk Doctrine, is as follows:

1. Whenever there is a feeling of concern or uncertainty in your gut, the nagging feeling that something just isn't *right*, ask the three questions to yourself and/or the group.

2. If the first two answers are affirmative, and there is a raging discussion or debate about how close you are to Big Risk, then this is the exact moment to make the first

meaningful course correction. Stop yakking! Take action! Now!

3. Keep making course corrections until you are sure you have sidestepped the Big Risk.

When dealing with Big Risk, the key ingredients to landing safely are that we recognize the risk itself and make the first meaningful course correction in a timely manner. To land safely every day, both pilots *and* parents recognize they must avoid Big Risk and not fly *toward it*. From my observations, this may apply to organizations, businesses, societies, and species.

We will never defeat Big Risk. That is a pipe dream. But if we work together as a united American team (or global team), I am confident we can safely fly past it again. And in this book, I will show you how the techniques I have observed, learned, and developed over the past four decades in the cockpit can help us do just that.

"Fly safe."

—CAPTAIN BRAD BARTHOLOMEW

PART ONE: WISDOM FROM THE COCKPIT

Chapter One:

FLYING CHANGES EVERYTHING

"Truly superior pilots are those who use their superior judgment to avoid those situations where they might have to use their superior skills."

—Frank Borman, pilot, astronaut and Apollo 8 commander

In the mid-1980s, I was an instructor in the United States Air Force teaching student pilots to fly. Those years were the most rewarding and the happiest of my forty-year career as a pilot, probably because the students I taught were routinely so damn capable. Although they were in their early twenties at most, these student pilots were some of the best and brightest of their age-group—intelligent, dedicated, and, most of all, hungry for knowledge. They wanted to learn everything imaginable about the aircrafts they were learning to fly, they were bubbling over with questions, and they took everything seriously. In short, they were an instructor's dream.

Although they hadn't honed their techniques yet—that was where I came in—these young pilots had a legitimate passion to learn how to get a plane safely in the air and down on the ground, and they really wanted to excel at their chosen profession. As a result, I truly looked forward to each new challenge I helped these students tackle. It was a magical time, one that made me feel I had a real purpose in life—and an important one at that. I may have been only twenty-four or twenty-five years old myself at the time, but it was clear that those pilots looked up to me, and I knew it was my responsibility to make them into the aviators they wanted to become, a responsibility I took seriously.

Maybe I'm romanticizing things a bit—actually, I know I am—because I sure wouldn't have thought about my job in such glowing terms on the mornings where I was scheduled to take off at 5:15 a.m., spending much of my day making sure the two rookie students in the cockpit didn't kill each another! But being a good mentor was important not only in terms of the education I was imparting to my students, it also helped make me into the pilot I am today.

Essentially, the relationship between a student pilot and an instructor is the same type of dynamic which often motivates most educators as well as parents. I may have been young myself, but there was no denying that I was in a paternal role—these kids were my flock. Many of the students had gone from college straight into the pilot training program, which was a year-long series of hurdles with another six to twelve months of flying their particular airplane after they'd passed all their requirements and been handed an assignment. After that, they were facing a commitment of another six or seven years in the Air Force performing their assigned mission. It was my duty to guide these young men through the process and help mold them into the pilots I knew they could one day become.

Back then, pilot training began in a T-37, an extremely forgiving aircraft, one that is only capable of flying around two to three miles per minute, which is practically crawling in aviator speak. Those beginning instructors had a tough workload, since they were responsible for taking a brand-new student who had never flown before and teaching them basic concepts of aviation such as how to take off, how to land, how to fly next to another plane, and how to perform a loop. But since I was a T-38 instructor, I'd get those same students around six months after they'd already learned to fly the T-37, when the basics were already under their belt.

Now, in comparison, the T-38 flies at seven, eight, or nine miles per minute, so it's a much faster plane overall. I didn't have to teach the students any new maneuvers—they had learned all of them before they ever stepped foot in the cockpit of the T-38. My only job was to retrain a student's brain, rewire it from being comfortable with flying at two or three miles per minute to handle flying at a nine mile-per-minute clip. Ultimately, and as all pilots understand it, the only difference between flying those two planes is how fast your brain can process information, and sometimes the students really struggled with these differences. It was a challenge as an instructor as well, because unlike the T-37, not only is the T-38 faster, but in the T-38, the instructor sits behind the student, as opposed to side by side. If a problem arose, I couldn't just reach over and deal with it as easily.

Looking back on those days, I can't help but remember one particular student. He was like so many of the other young men I'd taught before him: bright, dedicated, and ambitious. On paper, he had everything it takes to excel as a pilot: a great attitude, a solid set of the necessary skills, and, maybe most importantly, the drive and hunger to succeed. In the initial stages of our work together, it seemed as though he'd do just fine throughout the program. But in the middle of his training, I left on a long-awaited vacation, and in my absence, things fell apart spectacularly. Just before I left, he was fast approaching one of the biggest hurdles in the pilot training program overall, one every rookie pilot both fears and looks forward to in equal measure: flying solo.

Now, I only heard about it after the fact, but something happened on that flight that essentially freaked that young pilot's head out, and as a result, he just couldn't seem to figure out how to land the airplane. Every time he'd come in for a landing, he'd reflexively pull back and go around again instead. He did this over and over, missing the landing every time. Now, when you're coming in for a landing, you're in a pattern, with an instructor pilot air traffic controller overseeing. In this particular instance, the young pilot kept saying, "I can't do it I can't do it," becoming more and more frustrated and unsure with every missed landing. Finally the instructor on the ground was able to talk him down, and the pilot landed the plane successfully. But by time I returned from vacation a week later, the student had decided to quit the pilot training program altogether.

When I met with him, I remember sitting there, trying to keep an impartial expression on my face, but inside I was stunned at the words I was hearing out of his mouth. He kept saying, "I don't think I was meant to be a pilot," repeating it over and over while shaking his head "no" emphatically. I stayed calm and just listened, and then when he was through explaining, I tried to reassure him, as instructors are taught to do. I told him that every rookie pilot has moments of fear in the air and that he could get past it, that we could face that fear together and conquer it.

But I could tell by the look in his eye that my words were falling on deaf ears. No matter what I said, he just kept repeating that he couldn't do it, that he wasn't cut out for flying. And that was it. We're taught as instructors that once a candidate says he's done, he's done—you don't ever force them to fly if they've said repeatedly that they don't want to.

The fear that young pilot felt in the air? That sense of dread that resulted in his inability to land the plane initially? It's completely normal, and part of the process of learning to fly. But it's how pilots *respond* to that fear that matters. The fear itself is merely the recognition that (a) you're scared, (b) you have a problem, and (c) you don't know what's going to happen next. But the simple fact is that any one of these thoughts has the ability to bring a pilot to the same conclusion: it's showtime. And in those moments, pilots have to act—and quickly at that. One of the reasons pilots function well under extreme stress is because of the vast amount of training we endure. But this trainee hadn't had enough hours in the air as of yet, and, as such, hadn't been pushed past the notion that a pilot *can* get scared in the air, he hadn't gotten past the idea that even if he did experience moments of fear, that a pilot can *still* manage to push *through* that fear and problem-solve effectively. And who knows? There may have been something missing in that young pilot's psyche that ultimately made him a poor candidate for the job; he may have simply lacked the necessary ability to adequately handle extreme stress.

A friend recently told me a story that I feel perfectly illustrates my point regarding how people routinely handle extreme stress and the fear it causes. On a recent outing, I commented that she was a very good driver. She laughed and told me that it hadn't always been the case. "I was in a terrible car accident years ago," she told me. "The car rolled and caught on fire and I was trapped inside. Eventually I was rescued, but I'd broken my back and had to wear a brace for six months. After that I developed a real, paralyzing fear of driving. Every time I'd try to get behind the wheel and so much as coast down the driveway, I'd have a panic attack. I'd start hyperventilating and gasping for air. So for around three years, I just didn't drive. My husband and I lived in a small town in the Midwest where it wasn't completely necessary, so I didn't have to face my fear at all. But then I got a job in California, in the city of Palos Verdes, and I took it."

"How did you get away with not driving in California?" I asked, bewildered. Now California is a wonderful place to visit and to live, but unlike cities like New York or Chicago, public transportation is not its strong suit.

"That's the point. I didn't," she said as she smoothly turned left. "We were living in Long Beach at the time, and in order to get to work in Palos Verdes every day I had to drive across a huge bridge that terrified me. I don't know what I was more scared of, driving in general or that bridge, but it was a close tie. At first, I asked my husband to drive me to work each day. But he soon grew exasperated with my inability to really deal with the situation effectively.

One Saturday after lunch, he turned to me out of the blue and said, 'This has gone on long enough. Come Monday morning? You're driving yourself to work.' I protested of course and was completely indignant. But knew I didn't really have a leg to stand on.

So we got in the car and I drove across that bridge—not once but over and over again. At first, I was shaking and sweating, my heart racing every time I saw that giant steel structure looming up ahead. My fingers gripping the wheel were white with fear. But the more I did it, the less I felt anything at all, including nervousness, panic, or fear. My husband talked to me in a calm voice, reminding me of the tasks I needed to perform to drive effectively and safely: to check the mirrors, signal when changing lanes, and to keep my eyes trained on the horizon when crossing the bridge and not look down. As I performed each task, focusing on the hum of the engine and the music playing softly on the radio instead of my own fear, the panic began to recede little by little, and by the time the late afternoon sun was setting over the water, I was driving across that bridge as if it had never been a problem at all."

What my friend was able to do was to lean on her co-pilot, her husband, so she could problem-solve under stress, which is a skill pilots utilize every day in the air. Her husband, like any good instructor, knew that all she needed was a little push, coupled with a confidence boost of being able to drive successfully, to face her fear.

What she experienced behind the wheel that day was one of the most important things I've learned in all my years as a pilot: *flying changes everything.* It crystallizes the consequences, the risks involved, and the need to effectively problem-solve. Like my friend who successfully learned to drive across that bridge, once we mentally click over to the idea that we need to problem-solve, then problem-solving itself becomes paramount to what we do—which immediately tamps down the intense emotions of anxiety flowing through our bodies.

In these moments, we often feel intensely startled, but we pilots have learned throughout years of training that giving in to emotions that overwhelm us isn't exceedingly helpful. In fact, it is at these exact moments that we begin problem-solving in earnest. While many of us might freeze up at such times, seasoned pilots, however, have already mentally completed steps one and two: *yes, we have a problem and yes, it is our job to solve it.*

Risk and Time

Even though I'm now a seasoned pilot with many years of problem-solving experience under his belt, it wasn't always the case. I once found myself in a similarly nerve-racking situation as the young pilot I mentioned previously. It was a regular day in the air, much like any other, and I was engrossed in the task of teaching the student pilot I was working with a series of confidence maneuvers. To begin the one maneuver in particular we were focusing on that day, the student was asked to accelerate to three hundred knots and then pull the nose up to sixty degrees above the horizon. If performed correctly, as the plane zoomed upward, the airspeed would slow and the control stick would be pushed forward causing zero gravity. The plane would then essentially fly in a large parabolic curve. As the nose went below the horizon again, the airspeed would once again increase and the confidence-building maneuver would be complete.

On one particular training flight—that is still vividly seared into my brain—the student was a little reluctant to pull the nose upward during the maneuver. After a few minutes of hesitation, I began to coach him verbally. "Get the nose up!" I urged him repeatedly. At the next inopportune moment, I allowed my coaching enthusiasm to overwhelm my attention to the problem at hand, and as a result, the student jerked the nose straight to the sky. Instead of the nose of the aircraft being sixty degrees above the horizon and in a controlled flight, we were now flying straight toward the sky, rapidly losing airspeed and entering an uncontrollable flight pattern.

I instantly took over the controls, but the problem was that I wasn't in control of the aircraft. Moments later, we zoomed out of the top of the practice area as the airspeed was rolling back and the nose was still pointed straight up. Just to make this flying experience more interesting, a scan of the engine instruments revealed they were producing no thrust. It was also eerily quiet. This had now officially escalated into a stressful, "OH SHIT" type of moment, the kind that causes one to panic. For a nanosecond, the normally powerful T-38 hung suspended in the air, motionless pointing upward; then the nose violently flopped straight down. Now—from somewhere six miles above Arizona—time seemed to enter an unfamiliar dimension of hyper-speed.

Back then, the memorized procedure to restart the engines was to accelerate and push the throttles up to full afterburner. At this split second, my airspeed was zero, but at least I was now pointing at the ground. At the very next moment, the altimeter started spinning as we headed downward, but my airspeed indicator seemed to accelerate at an agonizingly slow pace.

The T-38 does have ejection seats, and the thought of punching out did cross my mind. "Punching out" is pilot lingo for squeezing the ejection handles, firing the explosive charge under the seats, which will eject the pilot from the plane so he may parachute to safety, leaving the plane to crash and be destroyed.

After making a quick calculation of the altitude below me, acceleration rates, and airspeed, I rejected the ejection option and stayed focused on the current conundrum. Truth be told, pilots will recognize my keen and calm calculation as a WAG, or a wild-ass guess. In a few more nanoseconds the engines roared back to life, but I still had to make one more mental calculation … or WAG. The best cornering velocity of the T-38 was about four hundred knots. As the earth was coming increasingly in focus and time slammed into light speed, I patiently waited—perhaps a split second or two—until the airspeed indicator read four hundred. At that instant, I snapped a pull of seven G's on the nose of the aircraft, bringing our flightpath back up to the horizon. As a result, we returned to stable level—straight-and-level flight at four thousand feet above the ground. The plane was safe. We stepped on solid ground a bit shakier than before takeoff, but essentially unharmed.

This event happened over thirty-five years ago, and the entire confidence-building maneuver probably lasted only eight or ten seconds, but I have never forgotten the lessons learned from the mistakes I made that day. They were seared into my brain in those crucial moments where things could've gone very, very wrong indeed. And because of the fact that my brain was most likely rewired by the stress of this event, I never forgot it. In hindsight, I probably lost my cool for only two to three seconds, but it took every ounce of my skills—not to mention a considerable amount of brain power and the effective management of stress—in order to recover safely. At the end of the day, the reality of life has many dynamic and imbedded forces that often collide with one another. When flying an airplane, two of these forces—risk and time—must always be respected.

My point in telling you the above story is that I firmly believe that a pilot is built, not born. Pilot training in general is an extremely expensive endeavor. So much goes into the creation of a successful pilot, and one piece of the puzzle is certainly financial. Thirty-five years ago, it cost around a million dollars per candidate to train a transport pilot, and four million dollars to train a fighter pilot. Back in the day, my particular class of trainees had thirty-four candidates at the outset. By the last day, only twenty-four men remained. In 2020, it may cost ten times that amount to put a candidate through an entire course of pilot training.

On top of this, the equipment itself is extremely expensive to both operate and maintain. Heck, the plane just on its own runs around ten million dollars. In World War II, President Roosevelt got it into his head to try and build forty thousand planes a year. We never approached anywhere near that number, but we did wind up killing more pilots in training than in combat simply because the recruiting standards in place were so minimal. Although it is undoubtedly the vast amount of training a pilot receives that makes him or her successful, there is something ineffable that sets pilots apart from mere civilians with flight dreams. The problem is that no one is exactly sure what it is yet.

In the mid-1980s, pilot training began to be so prohibitively expensive that people decided to study successful aviators to determine exactly what made one person a better pilot candidate than another. Was there some special pilot gene that some folks routinely possessed? Some factor in a candidate's psychological makeup that made him more predisposed to excel at the job than someone else?

Many years ago when I was living in the Washington D.C. area, one of the high-powered consulting firms in the area began studying pilots and performing psychological tests on volunteers—mostly aptitude tests. I thought the premise sounded interesting, so I volunteered for the two-day program. For a day and a half we endured around fifteen different tests, and when they were completed, I approached the instructor at the front of the room, who was busily shuffling a stack of papers in front of him. "Hey," I said, genuinely curious about the results, "so what did you guys find out?"

"Not much," he answered with an apologetic chuckle. "The only thing that we can correlate had to do with one particular task we gave you guys. The hole punch test."

I knew instantly what he was referring to. There had been one exercise where the instructor had held up a blank sheet of paper in front of us, then he grabbed a hole punch and folded the piece of paper in half. He then proceeded to punch a hole in one corner and asked, "When I open it up, where will the two holes be?" In the second round, he proceeded to fold the same paper in half again . . . and then folded it in half one more time. He then punched a hole in the folded paper and asked if we knew where the four holes might show up. The third time, the instructor folded the paper in half again, then folded it *twice* more and asked the same question: "Where will the eight holes be?"

"When we do this test with the average person," the instructor told me, "Most people flunk in the second or third round."

"Really?" I answered, unable to keep the surprise from my voice. I'd thought the exercise relatively easy.

"Yep," he said with another little laugh. "And *you're* a particularly interesting case. You flunked out in the seventh round—and you were absolutely *furious* with yourself for doing so." He stopped for a moment to gauge my reaction, which was probably stunned in that moment, before continuing. "It seems like you pilots," he went on, "can see things in 3D that the rest of us only experience in two dimensions."

I stood there for a minute, letting what I'd just heard sink in. What that instructor was referring to is what we pilots know as energy management, a concept taught across the board in pilot training. In order to explain what energy management is and exactly how it works, I offer the following scenario. If I'm flying straight and level at four thousand feet approaching an airport, the energy I have in that plane is directly related to the power I have in those engines. And as I approach the field for a landing, the configuration of my plane is clean, the gear is up, and flaps are up. The plane is very aerodynamic in that moment, but I know that as I approach the field, I have to put the gear and flaps down so I can slow down to a speed that is safe to land at.

To accomplish this, I need to pull back on the throttle to slow down so I can get the flaps down, but at the same time I also know that when I do so, I'll immediately have to push up the throttle to get more power to compensate for the fact that I'll be experiencing more drag. If I lose the power in that configuration, the plane will come straight down, and I won't glide very far. Now if you take that same plane and put it up at forty thousand feet, it's a completely different scenario. In that instance, I know I can bring the throttles back to idle and probably glide for another hundred miles. I have so much potential energy in that plane that I don't need the throttles anymore to come down. But at four thousand feet, that isn't the case.

So, circling back to that instructor's comment so many years ago in D.C., a pilot needs to be able to not just have the ability to experience what he sees in 3D, but to also *understand* what that *means*, and to ultimately be able to *problem-solve* in 3D as well. What I think that particular instructor was noticing was that pilots, unlike most of the general population, routinely develop the ability to see where they are going to end up in the future, and part of that ability is having an understanding of Situational Awareness.

What Is Situational Awareness?

Over the years, Situational Awareness has been called by a variety of names. Some may refer to it as simply paying attention, having mindfulness, or using common sense, while others may see it as having ingenuity or perseverance. If you ask several pilots about Situational Awareness, you will probably get several slightly different answers. All pilots know what Situational Awareness is, understand it, and can feel it, but we all use the term in our own unique way. Flexibility is one of its greatest assets. The traditional definition of Situational Awareness is the act of knowing what is going on around you. However, my personal belief is that this definition is a bit weak and incomplete.

Throughout my many years as a working pilot, I have seen a plethora of technology and software enter the cockpit and take up residence. Perhaps I am being snarky, but in my experience, version

1.0 of such gadgets quite never lives up to its hype or promises. Version 2.0 often fixes the "bugs" in version 1.0 but is still more annoying to pilots than helpful. By the time version 3.0 arrives, the gadget maker and gadget buyers have actually talked to pilots and asked them what they need to fly airplanes more effectively, efficiently, and safely. By the time the version 3.0 upgrade hits the cockpit, it has usually transformed into a quality product and something that is, in the end, quite useful.

But even when these fancy gadgets become a quality product, additional problems can surface. Over time, these remarkable gadgets can become mental crutches that pilots routinely rely upon without understanding what calculation is being performed or why. If this transformation occurs, then the gadget and the plane start flying the pilot. In aviation, compliancy is a dangerous fork in the road.

To that end, I will push the traditional definition of Situational Awareness further forward and redefine it as, "problem-solving under stress." These problem-solving tools and techniques can be used by anyone, by groups both large and small, and in any situation to accomplish tasks of any size or difficulty. Situational Awareness is also a useful tool to have at your disposal to strengthen relationships, but more on that in a bit. I would like to think my enhanced definition of Situational Awareness—problem-solving under stress—is also of version 3.0 quality and a useful upgrade.

When stress hits the cockpit, whether it is stress between the Captain and the First Officer or the stress of a particularly bumpy stretch of air, it has the ability to vividly impact and impair previous training, not to mention a pilot's thinking and communication skills. Just like what happened to me in the scenario mentioned above, and what probably occurred in the mind of the trainee pilot first discussed in this chapter, when stress hits, consequences of poor choices and a subpar performance become crystal clear in an instant. In the air, the reality of the situation has true meaning, not to mention deadly consequences. It is crucial to remember that *Situational Awareness is primarily a head game. So is problem-solving. So is landing safely. So are relationships.* This is true for a single individual, but it is also true for families, communities, work environments, societies, and the human race in general. Truth be told, Situational Awareness, and its enhanced version, could probably be best described as wisdom passed down by previous generations.

Now that I have defined two different definitions of Situational Awareness, I will focus on the task of understanding what is going on around us and how to deal with it—otherwise known as the act of problem-solving under stress.

Situational Awareness

Traditional definition: Knowing what is going on around you.

Enhanced definition: Problem-solving under stress.

Chapter Two:

FLYING CRYSTALLIZES RISK, RESOURCES, AND REALITY

"Experience is a hard teacher.
First comes the test, then the lesson."

—Vernon Law, Major League
Baseball pitcher

Flying can be stressful. Flying can be risky. Flying is dynamic. The reality of human life on earth is not normally this stressful, risky, or dynamic, but it can be. Flying high above the ground has a way of crystalizing everyone's focus. It also illuminates limited resources. While flying an airplane, the consequences of current actions are never far from the pilot's thoughts. This mental focus adds clarity and instantly discards bullshit. The sooner the pilots can grasp the facts and truth, the better we are able to deal with the reality of the situation. The facts and the truth are not always readily apparent while flying, but you can be damn sure the pilots are seeking to find them ASAP.

Another unique aspect of flying is that the pilots and their passengers have the exact same risk–reward profile. While airborne, the personal interests of the professional (pilots) providing the good and services and the personal interests of their clients (passengers) are perfectly aligned. Ultimately, we both have the exact same amount of skin in the game. More specifically, we have skin in *both* games—the upside and the downside. If we mishandle the aircraft and the plane crashes, we go down right along with it, just like our passengers. Perhaps this is why most people like pilots: we are Type A people who are trustworthy in the air, due to the fact that we need the exact same thing *every time*: a safe landing.

Even though all good pilots are aware of the fact that the perfect flight has never been flown, we also understand that failure is not an option. On the ground, stressful situations often change our bodily chemistry, producing an uncomfortable feeling. Being airborne greatly amplifies this anxiety, which is why it is important to understand how to recognize this stress, handle it effectively, and then let it go.

Here is how I deconstruct the three components of cockpit stress:

1. The environment is always changing. Each flight is unique and the weather is always subject to change. The dynamics of airports change, too.

2. Pilots generally have limited resources. The most unyielding resource is fuel, which equates to time. Both are fixed and finite. Power from the engines is fixed and finite, too. The flight characteristics of the airplane are limited, and

sometimes working capabilities of the instruments can be limited. The skills and training of the crew can be limited resources, too.

3. There aren't always good options—and we aren't automatically entitled to the good options we *do* have.

But aren't these same stress components present on the ground faced by all of us … people, pilots, and parents? Aren't these the same stress components faced by communities, businesses, and societies?

After all, don't we *all* need safe landings?

The Components of Problem-Solving under Stress

1. A lack of resources

2. A lack of viable options

3. A changing environment

Healthy Debriefs

But how do we land safely each time? As I explained in Chapter One, without the pressure and consequences of flying, the new pilot was able to objectively see his performance and recall what he was thinking during the execution phase. This is when understanding and learning occurs. This is how future performance is improved. The possibility of a safe landing greatly increases if there is a healthy debrief following each flight.

As an instructor, in the beginning stages of working with a student pilot, the first few things you impart to him are extremely basic in scope. But as time goes on, you begin to challenge the student with more and more complex instructions. Each time he is challenged, he also experiences more anxiety, but over time and with guidance, he learns to push through it. From then on, he has the confidence he needs to excel in situations where he is startled or scared, and that information is stored in his brain for later use, is hardwired, so to speak.

As I mentioned earlier, a perfect flight has never been flown. In the air, things happen so quickly that a pilot won't necessarily remember what happened or *how* it happened. But in a debrief, he will often start to recall the flight in detail, and as a result, the mistakes he made in the air suddenly become visible. He recalls with more clarity a moment where he could've performed a task a little more effectively. When a pilot is down on the ground and can finally relax, he has the ability to learn from his experience, so that he can hopefully do things a little bit better next time.

In the training environment, rookie pilots experience an extremely thorough debrief after each and every flight. But in the day-to-day life of a seasoned pilot, there's no formal debriefing process. In the air, events can unfold quickly. There are extremely rare instances, however, when the First Officer and I disagree on the desired course of action and I choose to override his assessment or judgement. If this happens, I expect my First Officer to be supportive and on board in that moment, and that our first priority will be to get the plane down on the ground. But after we land safely, I never forget that there was a difference of opinion or that his viewpoint differed from mine at a crucial moment. Now, I'm not going to discuss it in the air because in that moment we have work to do. But after the plane is safely on the ground, we're not flying again until we have a little chat. It's imperative as the Captain that my First Officer not only has his say, but that I really *listen to better understand what occurred so we can both* process it properly and move forward with a shared mental model. Most importantly, I need the reassurance that if, one day in the future, we get in another tense situation, he will have my back. If I choose to leave some significant issue or moment of conflict between us unresolved, the next challenge might have a very different outcome. One we might not walk away from so easily.

We debrief so that we can improve our performance the next time around. Each time a pilot performs a maneuver successfully, his confidence grows. By the third or fourth time he performs a once alien and stressful maneuver, it no longer feels as challenging, but more natural. And if somehow the situation changes and *becomes* challenging mid-flight, the pilot knows that he has the tools and experience to problem-solve effectively. Learning from past experiences is one of life's best teachers. I still mentally debrief myself after every day in the air. Properly debriefing one's successes *and mistakes* can be quite humbling but is a direct path to a career of safe landings. After all, the goal of a healthy debrief is to understand what happened and why, as the true purpose of a debrief is to improve future performance and results.

Part of the debrief is realizing just how important past experience really is. I remember that years ago, after our first child was born, there were times when I was completely terrified. Scared that if I even looked the wrong way at that tiny, defenseless little human, I'd somehow screw it all up irreparably. I remember the day that my wife and I left the hospital with our daughter like it was yesterday.

After we'd secured her in the tiny car seat, pulling the straps tightly around her soft, floppy body, so defenseless and tiny in that large, protective seat, there was a moment where my wife and I simply looked at each other in astonishment. "We have to ... keep her alive now?" she said, her tone almost incredulous. "It's not like they come with instruction manuals!"

In hindsight, this kind of new-parent paranoia was actually kind of funny, but at the time I knew exactly what she meant. I felt it viscerally in my body, that fear mixed with the fierce responsibility for that little person already snoozing and drooling in the back seat. Now, if my wife and I had continued to dwell on that fact, we may well have become paralyzed, unable to act or think effectively when our daughter needed us, which was constantly. And after a few days passed, and what had once seemed strange and foreign had now become the new normal, it became easier to push those moments of fear away and, instead, focus on problem-solving effectively. Loud wailing? Was her diaper wet? How long had it been since her last feeding? Did she have a fever? Did she need to be picked up and rocked?

And speaking of illness, a friend once told me that when her six-month-old daughter suddenly began running a temperature of 102, she rushed her baby to the hospital, praying under her breath the whole way that the infant would recover. After what felt like an interminable wait in the exam room, the attending doctor finally walked in, examined the child, and gave my friend a reassuring smile "It's just a virus," he told her, "Alternate Tylenol and Advil to break the fever, run a vaporizer in her room, and your baby will be just fine."

After that experience, as stressful as it had been for her, my friend wasn't *as* worried the next time her daughter fell ill with a cold or the flu. She was concerned, sure, but she didn't panic because she'd already *had* that first experience with childhood illness, and it taught her that not only could she handle whatever came next, but that *whatever* happened, *the baby was most likely going to be just fine.* From that day on, when illness struck, she had the confidence to focus on what she needed to do to make the child comfortable, and to problem-solve effectively thereafter. In fact, in the evenings, she and her husband would often debrief and make a plan for the next day's care and also discuss how they'd handled things that day, always being conscious to be gentle with one another, and to take responsibility for their actions when things *didn't* go smoothly in their roles as caretakers.

Which brings me to my next point. The number one mistake often made during a debrief is choosing to play the blame game instead of taking responsibility for one's actions. We've all been there, and starting a conversation with the words, "You didn't" or "You never" is, in my experience, an express train to Blamesville. Playing the blame game is simply the opportunity to create an alternate reality in order to fit a desired narrative, status, or outcome. Blaming others may feel good in the moment but is often a dangerous distraction from the real issues at hand. Placing blame is ultimately a way of lying to oneself. When faced with meaningful events in life, lying to oneself in the present moment has the ability to cause harsh consequences in the future.

There is one additional benefit of a healthy debrief. If a person has experienced a trying situation and afterward takes the time—in a calm environment devoid of stress—to understand what happens and why, then the person's mind is more easily able to let go of that stress and calmly focus forward again. Mentally, the stressful event is another lesson learned and quickly becomes ancient history.

The bottom line is that opportunities to learn meaningful lessons in life should never be wasted.

Healthy Debriefs

1. The goal of a healthy debrief is to understand what happened and why.

2. The purpose of a debrief is to improve future performance and results.

3. The number one mistake of a healthy debrief is playing the blame game.

Chapter Three:

STEP ONE—PUTTING VARIABLES IN YOUR FAVOR

"Complexity is the enemy of execution."

—Tony Robbins

Life, like flying, is a game which requires getting as many variables in one's favor as humanly possible. Although the stakes are often higher for me in the air than for those safely down on the ground, the principle is much the same and can be applied to just about every situation one might encounter in life. That being said, here are two techniques I use while flying to put as many variables in my favor as possible.

The first technique involves checklists. In the cockpit, most checklists are used to verify work has already been properly completed. Checklists are a routine part of flying—sometimes a little *too* routine. When the First Officer reads the checklist and I respond, we both already have the words memorized. Like everyone else in the world, when performing tasks which are habitual and routine, my mind has a tendency to wander. However, if I sense I am not properly paying attention when performing the checklist, I then stop where I am, and we start from the beginning.

In these moments, my mind has wandered, and I know it is not safe for me to proceed in a distracted mindset. In this scenario, stopping and restarting the checklist is an annoying distraction, but a necessary one. Sometimes, it is not my own mind that distracts me in such moments, but the presence of other employees—flight attendants, fuelers, and others—who all have plenty of work to complete before the plane ever leaves the gate. In completing their assigned duties, they often need to talk to the cockpit. However, no matter who interrupts me while I'm completing a checklist, I will again stop what I am doing and restart it from the beginning.

The act of performing checklists properly is not always the most expeditious path, but it puts many variables in our favor. It makes the day go more smoothly and helps to build a strong safety net. I have performed a million checklists in my career as a pilot, and in doing so, I have caught thousands of errors before they put me, my crew, and my passengers near any danger.

The second technique also involves dealing with a distraction or interruption, but unlike the scenario above, this interruption is always a welcome one. This kind of distraction normally occurs when rampers (otherwise known as baggage handlers) come to the cockpit. The rampers receive no formal training on the mechanics of the airplane or how anything works, but even so, sometimes one will come to the cockpit to tell me that something doesn't look quite right with the airplane. I then stop what I am doing and leave my seat to follow him or her down to the ramp to inspect the airplane I'm about to fly. In these instances, I do not send the First Officer. I go myself.

Over the years, I would say at least two out of three times, the issue we find doesn't concern me in the slightest. But no matter what I find—be it insignificant or quite important—I always turn to the ramper and thank him or her for bringing it to my attention. And, *I mean it.* I always have time to listen and talk to people who are trying to help us all be safe. Because the fact of the matter is that undetected problems on the ground rarely become friendly problems in the air, and the sooner I can be alerted to bad news, the better are my chances of handling the concern without a lot of fuss, and perhaps more importantly, the better are my chances of smoothly navigating around Big Risk without getting hurt. Being open-minded enough to welcome bad news *early* may be the most powerful tool in gaining Situational Awareness in a timely manner.

Working in and around a grounded airplane can be a busy environment, but I always welcome interruptions when there is a safety concern—that is how we, working together, help mitigate any impending disaster.

The Divert Decision Tree

Even with proper Situational Awareness and a minimum of distractions, flying a commercial airliner in a scenario when something has gone wrong can quickly become chaotic and complex. As the Captain, the only thing I know for sure is the fact that I will have to deal with it. There is no pause button in the flying game. The first purpose of this story is to deconstruct complexity. Second, I will demonstrate several helpful Situational Awareness tools: identifying

Big Risk, prioritizing plans, and having a shared mental model. Now, I'm aware of the fact that most readers have never had the experience of flying an airplane, but I ask you to put yourself into this story as a flying passenger, one who will either reap the benefits or suffer the consequences.

The Divert Setup

Before each flight, the airline's dispatcher creates the flight plan, and the forecasted weather at the destination airport is always scrutinized. If that weather is worse than anticipated, an alternate landing airport is designated. Next, the required fuel to first fly to the desired destination (Plan A) is calculated, and then to the alternate airport (Plan B). On top of these calculations, a legally required amount of reserve fuel is also determined (Plan C). This total calculated amount of fuel is then loaded on the airplane. The divert decision tree emerges when the weather at the original destination airport deteriorates precluding a landing, and the plane must divert, meaning it must fly to an alternate airport to land safely.

In this story, Plan A is a plane which is flying into a busy hub destination airport. But airplanes are flown in a dynamic environment and sometimes things change. Just like life. To simplify, Plan A is our desired destination. However, if after takeoff, flying to the desired destination becomes unworkable, I need fuel onboard to fly to an alternate airport, otherwise known as Plan B. If Plan A and Plan B both fail, Plan C, using reserve fuel, becomes the last available option. Plan C is the survival, or Big Risk, plan—commonly referred to as the last resort.

Execution Phase

We are now flying toward our original and intended destination after an uneventful takeoff. About one hour away from our scheduled landing, we get an updated weather report indicating our destination weather is deteriorating, but still well above our required weather minimums. Unfortunately, thirty minutes from our destination airport, the air traffic controller suggests we slow down and expect to be put in a holding pattern. When we are at the outermost distance from the field, our onboard radar begins to give us a glimpse of what weather phenomenon is actually affecting the airport where we were originally scheduled to land.

Immediately, a mental checklist of several Situational Awareness questions surfaces: Why are we holding? Is it because of congestion of airplanes having to fly instrument approaches because of the low visibility? Has our arrival corridor closed? Are other arrival corridors closed, too? Have the tower controllers changed the landing runways to the opposite direction, because of a wind change? Has another aircraft tried to fly an instrument approach and not been able to land? Is there currently another aircraft on final approach trying to land? Has bad weather effectively closed the airport to all landing traffic?

For the sake of storytelling brevity, I will not explain each of the possible scenarios. I'll just state the answers to how each one of these questions—if I get answers—will impact my thinking, assessments, and actions. And just to amplify this uncomfortable feeling and complexity, at this exact moment there are maybe several dozens of other pilots, air traffic controllers, and dispatchers all facing this same dilemma, each with slightly different divert fuel capabilities/concerns. We pilots affectionately call this the "cone of confusion."

Work-Arounds, Assessments, and Ingenuity

I have a friend who works as an on-site project manager for a construction company. He often mentions that problems frequently arise when supplies fail to arrive on schedule to the job site or when the design doesn't work exactly as planned. Or, in rare instances, when a piece of equipment becomes inoperable. When these moments occur, as project manager, my buddy routinely assesses the problem in order to make a direct observation, listens to the concerns of the crew, asks a few probing questions, and then figures out a way for the work to keep moving forward. He calls this *a work-around.*

Even if a project *was* proceeding smoothly, at least once a week he still takes the time to step back and assess and reassess the job from all angles. In doing so, he purposely leaves his cellphone in his job site trailer and walks across the street, where he can view the project at a distance, but no one can access him. He then spends at least thirty minutes asking himself the following questions. First, what was the crew doing? Why were they doing it? How were they using their materials and resources? What adjustments could be made to smooth out the current rough spots? Then after reflecting on these questions, he mentally switches gears and challenges *himself* to think ahead. What reasonable outcomes could he expect, he asks himself, and is there a better path forward toward the desired outcome?

This friend mentioned one day that he learned this technique over forty years ago from his first union boss. He recalls that his first mentor used to always remark, "Every project worth doing right is going to need some 'Yankee ingenuity' to get to the finish line. And that will require you to use your brain, son."

Interestingly, I recall hearing the word "ingenuity" often in casual conversation constantly in my childhood and when I was a young pilot. However, in the past fifteen or twenty years, I haven't encountered the word much at all in daily life or polite conversation. Maybe it's time we brought ingenuity back into our vernacular. Because ingenuity is not only an integral part of developing good Situational Awareness techniques, it is also part of being able to navigate safe landings, both in the air and on the ground. But how do we do so when it seems that distractions and annoyances lurk around every corner?

The KISS Principle

This KISS principle was reportedly first coined by one of our most brilliant military aircraft engineer designers, Kelly Johnson, in the early 1960s. It stands for Keep It Simple, Stupid. Over the years, the acronym has gone through many variations. James Carville twisted it a bit during Bill Clinton's 1992 presidential campaign when he famously stated, "It's the economy, stupid."

One way to keep it simple—and not get dangerously distracted—is to determine what exactly *is* the biggest risk? In the scenario I mention above, I have a limited amount of fuel (and therefore flying time) to find a runway that is safe to land at. The Big Risk I'm facing now is running out of gas as I am flying toward *any* suitable runway. In pilot speak, I am now calculating my BINGO fuel. BINGO fuel is the amount of fuel that I must have when I discontinue flying toward the desired Plan A airport and turn and fly toward the Plan B airport. Making this calculation accurately ensures I will make a timely decision and take the appropriate action.

From past experiences, here are a few meaningful things to consider. First, if the Plan B airport is a standard alternate for a big hub airport, how many other airplanes will be aiming for that same destination at the exact same time I am? Further, if I am flying from the west to the east, this is also the direction that almost all weather fronts normally follow. If my Plan B legal and compliant alternate airport is east of my destination hub airport, then the same destructive weather that is hindering my arrival to the Plan A airport may also be challenging my diverted flight path to the Plan B airport.

Yup, these scenarios of snafus happen all the time. Life, more often than not, just isn't fair—we often have to choose from a series of tough choices that can make us feel uncomfortable. But our job is to learn how to deal with these uncomfortable choices—safely. This hypothetical story may explain why so many pilot debrief sessions end up at a bar, with pilots huddled in groups over a few beers—or in my case, bourbon.

During this cone-of-confusion period, the Situational Awareness mind must guard against a couple of mental traps. First, the current conditions at the Plan A airport have nothing to do with calculating the fuel needed to fly to the Plan B airport. Remember my job—at this moment—is to mitigate the Big Risk, not make everyone happy.

Second, in the original flight plan, there is a reserve fuel line item—but all the fuel onboard has real meaning now. To truly push back Big Risk, I must resist using any assigned reserve fuel in my calculations for a possible diverted flight to the Plan B airport. Reserve fuel is reserved for Plan C, which we will examine in a later chapter.

Now, let us step back from our real-life scenario and review our thought process. Why did we do all this Plan B prep work when our job and intentions were to land at the airport in Plan A?

Reason #1: We did all the Plan B prep work because we identified our biggest risk—diverting without enough fuel to get there and land safely. We mentally attacked that risk and took action to keep it far away from us. This is the key ingredient in practicing successful Situational Awareness techniques and securing a career of safe landings.

Reason #2: Now that we have engaged our brains, prioritized, and pushed the Big Risk away from us, we can now confidently return our full attention and focus on landing at the intended destination, Plan A airport. If the opportunity safely presents itself, we now have positioned ourselves in the best possible manner for a successful landing at our Plan A airport—which is what the paying passengers want and what I want to deliver to them, if possible.

Hand-flying an instrument approach into a hectic, low-visibility airport is really not that difficult for a properly trained, seasoned pilot. Actually, it can be rewarding and enjoyable! On the other hand, however, flying an instrument approach into an airport with unstable weather conditions and *not knowing whether you have enough fuel to safely divert to another airport is a living hell.*

So, what's the lesson here? When things look dicey, we *move away* from Big Risk and choose the option with the *least amount* of potential danger attached to it. This means relying on our Situational Awareness skills we have developed over time so that we do not become vulnerable to annoyances and distractions when the matter at hand needs our full attention.

A Shared Mental Model

Even though the above story was narrated from my perspective and my perspective only, the reality is that on every plane there are always two fully qualified pilots seated in the cockpit. On a real flight, we would *both* be ratcheting up our Situational Awareness in such a scenario, and the First Officer and I would be working together as a high-performance team. In fact, step one—at the first sign of confusion—is to designate who is flying the airplane. Step two is to designate which problems or tasks each member of the team is responsible for. Step three is to designate which radios each one of us will use.

Effective communication under stressful situations is a real challenge and vital skill. Again, at these crucial moments, what is in our heads matters greatly. The bottom line is the Captain and the First Officer must talk to each other enough—and question each other enough—to be confident that they understand both the situation and the execution plan in exactly the same way. We call this having a shared mental model, and it is another Situational Awareness skill that propels us precisely toward safer landings. When two parties share a mental model, there are no winners and losers—everyone is on the same team. In fact, these words don't even come into play. After all, when my First Officer and I manage to land safely in a thunderstorm, we don't pull up to the gate and think, "Wow, we really beat that thing!" On the contrary. We simply did our job to the best of our ability, focused on the task at hand (getting out of the bad weather pattern without incident), and landed the plane safely. We didn't triumph over Mother Nature or "beat" her. Instead, we worked *with* her—*and each other*—in order to get the plane down on the ground safely with our passengers intact. In these scenarios, winning or losing is verbiage that doesn't even come into play.

This idea can also be applied to other areas of life, such as marriage. I once confided in a friend about an argument I'd had with my wife, one that threatened to erode the very fabric of our relationship. "There's no winning those kinds of arguments, you know," my friend said quietly. When I protested, he said something that stopped me in my tracks. "Do you know what winners get in these kinds of arguments," he asked. I sat there wordlessly, waiting for him to continue. "Divorce papers," he finished, a small smile playing at the corners of his lips. And as I sat there, his words slowly sinking in, I realized that he was right—no one actually "wins." There is only collateral damage.

Not only does fixating on the idea of winning derail our Situational Awareness and our forward focus, it often makes communication and understanding downright impossible. Healthy debriefs are only possible in a nonthreatening environment, one without too much tension, judgment, or strife. And make no mistake, it is in the debrief where we learn from our mistakes, thus improving our chances of safer landings—of all kinds—in the future.

Debrief: The Divert Decision Tree

1. Complexity is the enemy of execution.
2. Under stress, Keep It Simple … Don't Be Stupid.
3. Never ignore Big Risk.

A shared mental model means that everyone understands the *situation* and the *execution plan*. In order to create a shared mental model, all parties involved need to talk to one another and ask questions to confirm that the group is indeed all on the same page.

Chapter Four:

GETTING AHEAD OF THE AIRPLANE

"The most worthless part of the runway is behind you."

—Aviation wisdom

Many years ago, I directly asked legendary Southwest Airlines (SWA) CEO Herb Kelleher how often he made decisions based on the numbers rather than his gut. Smiling, he looked straight in my eye and replied, "At least forty percent of time, I go with numbers. Mostly, I rely on talking to people and watching what they are doing. This makes my gut smarter."

Like other Situational Awareness skills, being ahead of the airplane is not a place, but rather a product of mental focus and gut feeling. Neurobiologists report that gut feelings can originate in the conscious or unconscious parts of our brains. The older I get, the more I think this idea of *a gut feeling* is actually a reference to our subconscious mind. The more I am able to quiet my conscious mind and begin to *hear* my subconscious mind, the better my Situational Awareness becomes. This is because the environments we all experience in our daily lives are fluid, not linear, and the critical situations we face can quickly switch with a loud bang from being routine scenarios to chaotic ones. Life can also slide from tranquil to dangerous without so much as a murmur.

We pilots often critique ourselves by saying whether we are ahead of or behind the airplane. Remember that most jets are flying through the sky at a ground speed of four hundred to five hundred miles per hour; staying mentally ahead of the jet is the key ingredient to excelling at our profession. Being ahead of the jet is characterized by a calm, focused, and mindful state of being. But being behind the airplane is the exact opposite. It is a state of mental anguish, and as such, it can be quite dangerous. It's important to remember that flying requires physical dexterity, but mostly it is a head game.

So is life.

Focusing Forward

Being ahead of the airplane requires many different skills. First, both the eyes *and* the mind must be focused forward so the pilot can quickly visualize the opportunities, and/or the consequences, of current events as they are unfolding. Second, the pilot must quickly make accurate assessments of those unfolding events. Finally, the pilot must be able to critically think under stress. Good Situational Awareness requires the same skills.

While airborne, worrying about what has already occurred is a distraction—and loss of proper focus. When we are focused on what is in front of the airplane and how to deal with it, we will have the greatest impact on a safe landing. There will be a proper time to sort what happened before and why—the debrief.

Focusing forward, with good Situational Awareness skills, actually gives a pilot—or a person, or group of people—the ability to see into the future. This skill makes it possible to continuously determine whether one is accurately heading toward a desired goal. Thus, this forward-thinking vision enhances a person's ability to make timely course corrections.

For example, a few years ago, a pilot friend of mine was transitioning to a new airplane. As expected, on his first training flight in the new aircraft, his performance was a bit awkward. About halfway through the four-hour flight, the instructor pilot asked my friend, "Are your hands hot?"

Bewildered at the question, his response was: "Huh ... What?"

"Your hands are probably smoking hot, because your brain is so far behind this airplane that the only things your hands can grab onto is the exhaust coming out from behind the engines," the instructor said with a wry smile. What he meant by this, of course, is that if the pilot is mentally ahead of the jet, he is *flying* that jet. But if the pilot is *not* ahead of the jet, then the jet *is flying him*. In this case, the jet was flying the pilot, which is never the optimal situation to be in—especially in the air, where focusing forward truly counts, and a loss of Situational Awareness can be catastrophic.

Proper Training

Life marches on ... and so does technology. To focus forward and stay ahead of the game mentally, we must be open-minded enough to acquire and learn new skills. We also require proper training. If the new skill is noncritical, then digitized training—a bulletin or video—is incredibly handy, can often work wonders, and is the least costly option. In today's fast-paced and litigious society, however, this digitized training seems to originate from three separate sources, which can greatly impact its effectiveness.

If the digital training is written and presented by someone who has much experience in the new task or skill, then the bulletin or video is normally effective and appreciated by those in need. There are thousands of outstanding "how to" YouTube videos on the Internet. The most helpful ones I have seen have one thing in common: the creator has a wealth of experience in accomplishing whatever task is being demonstrated for the viewer.

However, if this virtual training is authored by someone with little or no experience in the new task or skill, then the video is often ineffective and largely incomprehensible to its audience. In this scenario, I am not demeaning the intentions or character of the inexperienced author; I am simply making an observation. For example, if an aeronautical engineer designs a new gadget for the cockpit that enhances its safety, he or she should probably not be the person to make the video explaining how to use it. The training video should be made by *another pilot* who has flown with the gadget and has experience using it.

However, there is a third source of "training material." This material is not training, not exactly, and it tends to piss people off. This professional-produced material is generally presented as "helpful training," but it is specifically designed to shift liability away from the boss or organization—and everyone knows it. Often the liability is shifted from the top onto the worker on the bottom via carefully worded, compliance directives. Again, I am not demeaning the intentions or character of the inexperienced author. These authors, who are almost always corporate attorneys, are simply doing their job. The subterfuge is initiated by the elite group who is paying them.

When gaining a new skill—one that *is critical to the success and safety* of a task, operation, organization, family, community, or society—a one-time instructional video is almost never sufficient training. Gaining critical skills that allow the person doing the work or activity to be focused forward and mentally ahead of the task requires proper training *before* attempting the task.

To better visualize this importance, consider the U.S. military. Before the military hands a new recruit a gun, bomb, missile, truck, tank, airplane, or submarine, the proper training program is essential, if not mandatory. This includes personal discipline, mental fortitude, and teamwork. In fact, everyone working around such devices or who is tasked to fix or transport these devices must be properly trained. The resumes of the volunteers entering our military do not include any of these skills or previous experience. This type of quality training can take a long time and is often extremely expensive. Proper training is also essential for the needs of our country. As a military veteran, I have my fair share of gripes about military service, *but nonetheless, I firmly believe the U.S. military provides some of the finest training in world.*

In learning a new critical skill, one must have access to quality training in order to excel, and one of the key ingredients to success is the ability to openly discuss these stressful situations with others who have already successfully navigated similar challenges. However, these conversations or debriefs, which pass along understanding and wisdom, must be held in a nonthreatening environment. Only in a nonthreatening environment will a person who is learning a new critical skill feel comfortable enough to ask the pertinent questions which will accelerate their own understanding and development. Being debriefed by a compliance officer, a supervisor, or a boss who has never done the actual work *does not count.*

This kind of on-the-job training component cements the ability to be mentally ahead. In the flying game, this is key. For example, our busy hub airports are each their own unique beast—think Atlanta's Hartsfield or Chicago's O'Hare or Dallas's DFW. The first time I fly into a busy hub, I am on high alert, and I will often ask my First Officer if he has been there before. If he has, it is a great relief to me. I may still be the Captain, but in this scenario, it is the First Officer, with his valuable experience, who is leading. The second thing I do while we are flying toward the busy hub is to scrounge around on my iPad for any training bulletins or videos. Experience and familiarity are important components to a safe landing, and if I'm unsure of my environment, I make sure to get familiar and comfortable with it as quickly as humanly possible.

In every proper aviation training syllabus, there is always the *mental hurdle* to overcome of the solo flight, or the first flight without the instructor present. These are the flights that really focus the mind and help to cement understanding. I am assuming almost all professions integrate similar mental hurdles, designed to focus the mind and develop the necessary confidence to succeed.

The Stupid Bucket

Experiences can be good, bad, ugly, or even dangerous. But if we debrief properly, we often gain a series of helpful lessons from the experiences we face in life. In my case, "ugly" experiences often happen when I'm not focused forward, which exponentially increases my chances of falling into the Stupid Bucket. The Stupid Bucket is kind of like a ditch on the side of the road. If a person finds themselves stuck there with a shovel in their hand, step one is to stop digging. Do not make the problem worse.

Below is another checklist of reasons of why I have ended up stuck, even momentarily, in the Stupid Bucket. However, just because I fall in doesn't mean I have to stay there long. Part of developing good Situational Awareness is having the ability to recognize where I am. If I recognize I am in the Stupid Bucket, the realization that I need to start moving forward again is the first step toward getting *out*. That recognition is the key, and it's the path *back* to Situational Awareness and mindfulness. At moments like these, it is imperative to not let ourselves be overwhelmed by big emotions such as anger, fear, or anxiety. Throughout the course of my life, many of the biggest mistakes I've made personally, both *in the airplane and on the ground*, have occurred when I've given in to big emotions such as anger, and allowed them to overwhelm me. This is because when we are angry, we are often distracted, and thus lose our ability to process data with an open mind.

For example, think about how many ridiculous arguments we may have had with our spouse or significant other, arguments that are generally focused around something small and seemingly insignificant—such as unloading the dishwasher. In these kinds of scenarios, is the argument—which somehow has stretched on for twenty minutes and is beginning to encompass almost every aspect of the relationship—*really* about the dishwasher and who unloaded it last? No, of course not. It's about whether or not you want to stay together as a couple!

But by continuing to let anger control the situation, the real crux of the argument can never be reached and defused. In these moments when anger takes the driver's seat, both parties are simply too distracted and emotional. In general, angrily wallowing in the Stupid Bucket is a disadvantageous—or even a dangerous— place from which to confront life, both in the air and on the ground. Keeping a cool head will help us redirect our attention and face forward again. This course correction can help restore our Situational Awareness, which provides the skills we need to effectively address the problem.

After all, it's not how many times a person falls down or is knocked down that determines whether they will succeed or fail. Success is only dependent on how times a person manages to *get up*. And in moments such as these, recognizing where one is, getting up—or leaping out of the Stupid Bucket—is crucial.

The Stupid Bucket Checklist: Getting Out

When mired in the Stupid Bucket, these three questions help regain proper mental footing. Once I ask myself, "What am I doing and why am I doing it," it usually alerts me to the fact I am off target and that I need to focus forward once again.

1. What am I doing and why am I doing it?

2. What should I be doing?

3. What's coming next?

Timely Course Corrections

However, simply realizing that we are in the Stupid Bucket and need to move forward isn't quite enough to significantly change our results. It is *also* necessary to assess our environment in real time as a situation is unfolding and to make *timely course corrections.*

One of my good friends is a successful trial lawyer who credits his courtroom success to his ability to adapt to a changing environment once the proceedings start. His firm is a large, top-shelf law firm, and his clients' opponents in court battles also tend to be represented by large, successful firms. Therefore, it is a given that both parties enter the courtrooms well prepared, with a detailed plan on how to best represent their clients in a high-stakes court battle. When the proceedings start, he always begins with his prepared plan, but while the hearing or trial is rolling along, he is also focused on how the case is *actually unfolding,* not how he'd prefer it to go or how he'd planned for things to turn out. He listens to the facts presented but simultaneously attempts to read the pertinent people in the room, as well as their reactions. By doing so, he is looking for an opportunity to adapt his plan to the case—not the other way around. According to him, months of preparation can be won or lost by swiftly adapting in the courtroom. This is what I refer to as a *timely course correction.*

Chapter Five:

PLANS, MENTAL RADARS AND SITUATIONAL AWARENESS

"In preparing for battle I have always found that plans are useless, but planning is indispensable."

—General and President
Dwight D. Eisenhower

Over the course of my career as a pilot, I have come to believe that many of our guidance edicts—processes, compliance procedures, models, ideologies, or belief systems—have become corrupted for several reasons. First, most of these guidance missives are written by well-intentioned people, but some authors have hidden agendas. If an agenda is purposely hidden, then its true motives aren't pure in nature, and as a result, performance will eventually suffer. Consequences of these manipulated agendas (narratives) are normally felt by the larger group doing the work, but not always by the smaller group of authors with power and authority.

Next, many of today's directives fail because they are too complicated, and as a result, workers possess a limited grasp of what they are doing and why. Without clarity and understanding, under stress, performance suffers. As I've mentioned in previous chapters, this can often occur when new technology is introduced.

However, it is not only the fact that directives are often too complex—they also bring with them issues of compliance. If the edict is written as a straitjacket, how will workers make any necessary adjustments—or what I refer to as course corrections. Compliance officers writing these edicts may successfully shift any liability away from their bosses in doing so, but the costs and consequences of this rigidity—specifically, the lack of flexibility to appropriately respond to a changing environment—strip the workers off their use of powerful, safer, and more productive Situational Awareness skills.

I have worked in environments where workers were instructed merely to comply, and where that compliance was outright demanded of them. As a result, workers under these regimes often become disillusioned and bitter. I have also worked in environments where employees were encouraged to solve the problems themselves. Workers in this environment quickly became motivated and skillful. Many employees, including myself, find that hard work in a problem-solving environment is actually enjoyable, and customers love dealing with people who understand what is going on and, as a result, can effectively deal with change.

Despite this harsh critique, I do believe today most plans are written with the best of intentions by good people. Edicts or plans, however, are just a starting point. It is the execution of those plans and the results they produce that matter the most. However, oftentimes, when such plans are presented by authority figures, they are often instantly branded, cheered, and sanctified as wise, righteous, and infallible. As I've said before, planning is indispensable, but the plan only gets you to the runway ready for takeoff. It's the flying and the landings *that count the most.*

In democratic systems, we-the-people do the work and, as such, function as the ultimate checks and balances against tyranny, misplaced righteousness, *and stupidity.* We-the-people ultimately bear the benefits, costs, and consequences of our collective actions. But make no mistake, the use of *good, Situational Awareness techniques* never allows us to forget that any meaningful task, activity, or goal by a group, whether large or small, is always a *work in progress.*

Mental Radars and Hard Questions

There are many different kinds of radars. Some are physical radars and mental radars. Some use data from the past, but most are focused forward. Most radars are scanned using our eyes but engaging *all* of our senses can also provide vital, irreplaceable information. It's commonly believed that as human beings, we possess five senses—sight, sound, smell, taste, and touch—but many researchers now believe we may have as many as *twenty-one* distinct senses at our disposal. I believe that when we effectively use all our five senses, we can develop an effective sixth sense: Situational Awareness.

But back to radars. The plane I currently fly has a radar which is located in the front nose of the aircraft. These "line of sight" radars can "paint" weather in front of the airplane for about a hundred miles. When I started flying years ago, these radars were used for both navigation and weather avoidance. They could detect ground contours and intense weather by simply transmitting a radio wave and detecting which signals bounced back. The original radars produce only a grainy picture that had to be skillfully interpreted, but the information they provided was often vital. Historically, this technology was first used in the defense of London during World War II.

A radar is an invaluable tool—especially when you are traveling through the sky at eight miles a minute. They can also be a vital tool while hurrying through life. When flying civilian airplanes, and navigating most life events, it is smart to keep our head up, so our eyes can properly function as an effective radar and we can be focused forward. In a hostile combat situation, however, mental and physical radars must be focused in all directions *simultaneously*—which makes the task infinitely more difficult and dangerous. Eyesight is often our best radar in any situation—and it is absolutely vital in threatening situations. When I am flying an airplane, I always have three radars, or focal points, working. The first focal point is directly in front of me—what my eyes can see out the front window and what my cockpit radar can "paint." This focal point—which presents lots of data points—covers the next fifteen to twenty minutes of flight.

But hang on—I misspoke. Luckily for everyone onboard, there are actually *six* working radars in the cockpit. Myself, and my First Officer, each has three. These six radars overlap, but each particular radar also tells a unique story—and that's a good thing!

The second and third radars are mental radars—with limited data points and more unknowns. The second radar is focused on what are the en route conditions—past what my eyes and the cockpit radar can currently see. Even though I do not have real-time information about these conditions, I will soon have to safely navigate this area, too. Again, in the search for reliable data, the most valuable information is often obtained from the radios. There is normally always an aircraft ahead of me and listening to their adventures helps me stay "mentally ahead of the airplane," which is my job.

The third radar is my continuous mental focus on the destination weather and events, which is where I must land the airplane safely. There are three phases of flight: takeoff, en route, and landing. Normally the most challenging and critical phase is landing, followed by the takeoff phase and then the en route phase. It does not always work out this way, but mentally this is what airline pilots normally expect and is emphasized in our training. Teachers and parents may simply call this paying attention. The math geeks might call it solving simultaneous equations. I call it critical thinking and using mental radars. The concept is the same—no matter what it's called—and it has been around since the beginning of time. Along with using radars while I am flying, there are three additional questions bouncing around in my simple brain:

1. How much will my current actions cost me?

2. What are the unintended consequences of these actions?

3. Based on my current actions, who will I become?

Whether I am flying an airplane or navigating the course of my life, I do not need to dwell on these questions. Being merely cognizant of them is often enough to maintain a proper focus, make timely course corrections, and keep unwanted surprises to a minimum.

The first question is simple, obvious, and straightforward. All actions always have costs associated with them. The costs could be money, time, relationships, or a myriad of different resources, but all actions have costs or tradeoffs. I am always stunned how often people, or groups of people, focus only on what they want and ignore the costs.

The second question is also simple, obvious, and straightforward, but again often ignored. Most actions have unintended, or unwanted, consequences associated with them. I am not saying that every unintended consequence of my actions is harmful or dangerous, but being cognizant of them—before I take an action—makes them much easier to deal with later on.

Question three is a corollary to question two but has stronger implications and more permanent consequences for my relationships. It's a difficult, self-reflective question that determines whether I am trustworthy or not. Notice that each of these questions is personalized. On the surface these concerns may sound a bit self-centered, but I disagree. I realize that the only person's action I can really control—on a good day—is my own. Also, asking myself these questions, before life unfolds, reminds me of a universal truth: there are always unintended consequences for myself and for others. Personalizing the questions also serves as a gentle reminder that I am still responsible for my actions, even if I am member of a larger group.

If I take ownership of my actions *and the unintended consequences*, people will gravitate toward me, not away from me. The same is true for owning my mistakes. I try not to make mistakes, but they happen. If I recognize a mistake, however, I can learn from it. If

I admit my mistake and own it, there is no need for people around me to point it out to me. There is no need to dwell on it either. All parties can continue to move forward. In doing so, I am attempting to demonstrate to myself and the people around me that my character, integrity, and trustworthiness do not change under stress.

My father used to say, "In the good times you'll have plenty of friends. It's navigating the bad times that counts the most. You can always tell who your true friends are because they'll stick by you in the bad times. Your job, son, is to be the type of person that people want to stand next to in both good times *and bad*. Life is so much easier and enjoyable when you have friends you can count on *and they can count on you*." In other words, trust is earned by actions, not words, and the full measure of trust is not fully solidified until we have navigated the bad times *together*.

I always keep these three radars and three questions in my head to help me choose the path I want to travel in life.

The Pivotal, Initial Steps of Situational Awareness

From my experiences and observations as a pilot, I find most efforts that become unattainable and/or unsustainable are hijacked from the start. The traditional definition of Situational Awareness, simply being aware of what is going on around you, points to this focus. If a person, or group of people, however, can get a firm grasp of reality by properly processing the credible and pertinent data and understanding the fundamental forces surrounding them, then they are off to a great start.

This immediate fork in the road we often encounter can have many different labels or signposts. Some of us see these two labels simply as success or failure. Others see these two paths as win-at-all-costs or sustainability. Still others read the signposts as morally, spiritually, ethically, or the ideology of right and wrong. In truth, these labels, names, or signposts are meaningless, but what matters significantly is *which path or road we choose.*

I have found over the years that the number one mistake in attempting Situational Awareness occurs at this initial fork in the road, and it is usually because we neglect to ask ourselves the following questions: Are we choosing a path that leads toward feeding a personal narrative, agenda, or belief system? Or are we choosing the path that, instead, leads to understanding and problem-solving?

Simply put, are we willing to play the cards we are dealt? Make no mistake, it is our *job* to play those cards. After all, we're not always dealt a good hand in life, and despite what we are often told or promised, we are never *entitled* to a good hand. Heck, if we are simply dealt a hand to play today, we should probably appreciate that fact and call it a good day! But how we play the cards we are dealt often determines our fate. This is why Situational Awareness techniques, or mindfulness, have been taught throughout the ages. But oftentimes, one path looks more inviting, whereas the other looks like ... more work. One path is generally seeking a firm grasp of reality and the other may not be. At this point, we must ask ourselves, "Do I want to be told what I want to hear? Or am I seeking out what I *need* to hear?"

In most stressful situations, I can easily be lured into lying to myself, which can feel comforting, but only in the short term. Searching for the information I need in order to make good assessments can be confusing, and often requires mental fortitude and perseverance to accurately resolve the issue at hand. This can require an inquisitive, questioning, and a probing focus, and will often lead to many uncomfortable realizations. Choosing this path often requires hard work, but it is generally the path to understanding, reality, and a career of safe landings.

However, I am not implying that it's an easy choice between the two paths. It can often be a mental wrestling match with oneself. Even now, after all my years of Situational Awareness training, in the initial stages of becoming aware of a challenge, task, or concern, I still often find myself reacting emotionally at those first moments.

My drug of choice is anger. Over the course of my career, I have been known to drop quite a few F-bombs in the cockpit. However, doing so is not necessarily always detrimental. A forceful outburst often serves to call the meeting to order, dispenses with old business, and focuses everyone's full attention on the sudden arrival of new business. My emotional outburst may take me a few steps toward the Stupid Bucket, but I do not stay there long, as the sudden arrival of new business items almost always requires problem-solving skills and timely execution. In short, as long as I keep facing forward and do not allow my anger to overwhelm me, I am on the right track.

All in all, it is important to remember the following when navigating life's challenges: life is, as a rule, dynamic. So is Situational Awareness.

Breaking the Disaster Chain

Most airplane accidents over the past fifty years are the result of six or seven completely random, seemingly unrelated events that tragically line up to bring down an airplane. We pilots call these the Swiss cheese accident model. These random events can happen to caring, capable people being distracted or in a hurry. These random events can be caused by someone who fails to perform a simple task properly or who simply refuses to stop their routine long enough to mentally recognize the fact that *something doesn't look right.*

Life on earth has an unpredictable, sneaky, chaos component. Sometimes several things just go exactly wrong at exactly the wrong moment. Such events can occur in any phase of the operation— planning, loading passengers, loading cargo, loading fuel, routine maintenance items; sometimes it's as simple as a missed item in a preflight checklist. Sometimes these events are the results of years of improper training or a lack of oversight, or simply a brief moment in time when someone failed to pay attention. Sometimes the root of contributing errors can be misplaced priorities, which often causes workers to be in a hurry. We all—the boss, employees, and customers—want that airplane to leave on time. That is our job. This is what we get paid to do.

The antidote to the Swiss cheese accident is called *breaking the disaster chain.* It means that an accident can happen when a series of simple variables tragically align. No one ever suspected these completely unrelated mistakes or simple oversights could perfectly line up at the exact same moment to cause an airplane to crash. Breaking this disaster chain can be as easy as noticing something out of place and thinking, *Hmm ... that doesn't seem right.* But here is the crucial step in this process, at these moments, we MUST, after noticing something is amiss, say something, *do* something, or *stop* what we were doing and *take the time to investigate more thoroughly.*

Bad things can—and do—happen to good, hardworking, well-trained, and caring people. That is why knowing what is going on around us and being vigilant and disciplined throughout the process are key ingredients in making sure bad things do not happen on our watch. That is how we take care of ourselves, our families, and each other.

Chapter Six:

GRIT

"Winning is one thing, but out of losing I always learned more. You don't waste time blaming someone else. Analyze yourself. Change yourself to be successful."

—Niki Lauda (Legendary World Champion Formula One Driver and pilot)

When I mentioned to a close friend of mine that I was writing about Situational Awareness, he excitedly relayed that he'd recently viewed a TED Talk, led by Professor Angela Duckworth of the University of Pennsylvania, that focused on the concept of grit. When I watched it, I was amazed by Duckworth's extensive research on the subject, and immediately bought her outstanding book, *Grit: The Power of Passion and Perseverance*, and read it cover to cover. The chapter you are about to read is the first of many instances where I will directly lean on the brilliant works of other authors and researchers who spend their lives deconstructing our humanity, as well as the particular ways in which we spend our time on earth. In preparing to write this book, I turned off the TV for the first time in years and was stunned to find so many fascinating works of nonfiction that seemed to speak to the exact concepts I was trying to develop. I'm sure this sudden turn of events frustrated my wife, as I was suddenly buying a new book each week.

The pejorative public viewpoint is that our media is both stale and hateful. Many are even of the opinion that not only is today's reporting biased, but it is also full of untruths, otherwise known as fake news. However, I think the reality of journalism today may, in fact, be the exact opposite. More specifically, I believe we are in a golden age of journalism and research. Furthermore, I strongly suspect that the fundamental question we face as a society may be whether there is a demand for illuminating and insightful information that is based on facts. Or are we, as a society, encouraging a pre-packaged message that speaks to the lowest common denominator? In democratic, capitalistic, and market-based societies, we-the-people control one of the most powerful levers on earth: *demand.* But the question is, which specific levers are we collectively choosing to pull?

Before I get back to *Grit,* I need to offer a huge disclaimer. I am responsible for my actions and words. If I misrepresent or misconstrue the valuable work of others, that is my error alone. When presenting the works of others, however, the most likely reality is I will realign their insights to fit my storyline. Since I intend to use this storytelling technique several more times and do not want to provide a wordy explanation each time, I will label this recurring technique as *Brad's storytelling disclaimer.*

For this literary tinkering, I offer no apologies. This kind of tinkering is, like it or not, how we work together constructively, building on each other's best ideas that often leads to improving our future performance. Our job and responsibility are not to make everyone happy. Our job and responsibility are not to arbitrage every single activity in the past to some negotiated, perceived, pristine level of justice. *If we want a healthy society tomorrow for our families, we need to work together today to improve our future performance.* In this context, the word *society* can be used in a community or workplace, and on domestic or global basis.

But before I get too far off-track, let's return back to *Grit*. One of Duckworth's first research challenges was to figure out why some young cadets at the army's West Point Academy made it through and thrived, whereas others failed and subsequently dropped out. Just like the young students I trained for the Air Force many years ago, these young cadets are some of our finest, accomplished, and supremely motivated young men and women in our country. Still, as I discussed previously in Chapter One, we instructor pilots never knew which students would succeed or fail until we got them in the air. Obviously, the same was true at West Point, but Duckworth's quest was to figure why.

Professor Duckworth initially interviewed all the new West Point cadets across a multitude of characteristics, accomplishments, and experiences and then tracked their progress over a course of months. Her research illuminated that the cadets who thrived were the ones who had persevered through previous rigorous challenges *before arriving* at the Academy. Their past experiences had taught them that when life knocks you down, the next step is to get back up. They had also realized that it's not if life will knock you down, it's when and how often. So be prepared.

The reason the school of hard knocks is such an effective teacher is because we often learn more from our failures than our successes. Grit, Situational Awareness, and confidence are skills and qualities that are earned, not simply passed out with a diploma. This is one reason I often shake my head in disbelief when I see helicopter parents continuously attempting to protect their children, at all costs, from experiencing some of life's most valuable lessons.

Duckworth labels this quality grit—the power of passion and perseverance. Her research also reveals that although not everyone possesses grit, it can be nurtured and taught, an idea that speaks strongly to Duckworth's personal passion in life and work. As she puts it, "Use psychological science to help children thrive."

As I see it, we need to utilize our experiences, observations, and training, along with wisdom gleaned from others, to better understand large-group dynamics. This way, we can work together to problem-solve, thrive, and land safely every day.

The True Meaning of Proper Training

While vacationing overseas a few years ago, my wife and were enjoying a pleasant conversation with a British couple. The husband was a medical doctor by profession but had been deployed several times to Iraq and Afghanistan as a reserve soldier. The first two times he was second-in-command of the medic units which were headed up by American officers. This specific type of unit was purposely deployed within close distance to fierce fighting in order to stop large amounts of blood loss in wounded soldiers and stabilize them for a quick helicopter ride to a military hospital.

On his third deployment, he learned he would be the commanding officer. Prior to the deployment, however, their newly formed international medic unit was flown to a predeployment training facility in Europe. There were about dozen medics in the unit, which included two other medical officers who were second-in-command—one was also a Brit and the other was an American. On day two of training, after hurling culturally laced as well as professional insults at one another all day, these two doctors nearly came to blows and eventually had to be separated.

As a result, their training was cut short, and the dueling doctors were dismissed for the day. Shortly afterward, my British friend calmly stood in front of the remaining group, took a deep breath, looked each member in the eye, and said, "I'm very glad this butting of heads happened here today. This training scenario is *designed* to be stressful, because the reality is the combat environment you will be thrust into in less than two weeks will feel ten times worse. It's now my job to get both of those two highly skilled physicians, who have not seen combat, back on our team." He smirked and chuckled a bit. "And that won't be hard—they both sound like I did a couple deployments ago."

After a debrief with the two feuding doctors, they were back on the same page and ready for any issues that might arise in combat. And sure enough, on that deployment, these men came under direct attack while caring for wounded soldiers. As a result, my friend had to give the command to the other physicians to get down and cover the three wounded soldiers with their own bodies for the longest five minutes of their lives. Without hesitating, everyone did their job without question, and got back to camp safely.

My point in relaying this story is that those who routinely work in operations know how to build teams that will perform effectively in most stressful situations. Meaningful training is not only essential, and each supervisor has their own unique way of leading, but all understand that we need grit and Situational Awareness in order to succeed and keep moving forward.

Debrief

Grit, Situational Awareness, and leadership cannot be freely given or assigned. They must be earned. Earning these skills builds the confidence to effectively deal with stressful environments. Unfortunately, earning this confidence can also lead to hubris, as well as inflated egos.

God-Like Captains

Aviation often learns its lessons the hard way, in horrific scenes of huge fireballs and human carnage. Along these same lines, we have also learned, again the hard way, about the two distinct paths that Captains can choose to travel. There is the problem-solving, team-building, safer path, and then, there is the overly confident, dangerous path, which is often full of bravado. In aviation, we often label the pilots who travel the second path as "God-like Captains." On the flight line, First Officers more descriptively refer to these pilots as "assholes, who won't listen to anyone."

When our industry was young, in the 1920s to 1950s, flying machines weren't very sophisticated or reliable. As a result, the act of flying these airplanes was often risky, and flying in bad weather or in combat was considered *extremely* dangerous. It took a certain type of person to climb into those unreliable machines day after day. These pilots had to literally fly *by the seat of their pants* in order to survive, and the only person they could rely on completely was themselves. As a result, these pilots became supremely confident, self-reliant individuals who became skilled in executing *the right stuff* at a moment's notice. Other than being fearless, what was in their head did not matter. But what they *did* mattered most. This period in aviation history produced the catchy industry phrase, "Flying is hours of boredom punctuated by moments of stark terror."

In the late 1950s, 1960s, and 1970s, airplanes became significantly more reliable as innovations in technology increased. These new birds transitioned from being built with wood and bulky steel to lighter-weight, stronger, steel and aluminum aircrafts powered by jet engines. As a result of these new design changes, airspeeds doubled or tripled, and the instruments in the cockpit significantly improved, too. Aircraft failures significantly decreased, and air travel become safer and more reliable. These quantum leaps in manufacturing and technology, however, did not prevent all accidents. The aircraft accident review boards detected there were problems brewing with the cockpit crews—specifically where the Captains were concerned.

It is a testament to the integrity of the aviation profession that we—as a supremely collaborative and safety conscious industry—have always aggressively investigated our failures. As an industry and profession, we have fearlessly searched for the truth, not to assign blame, but to understand and learn from our mistakes. The only purpose of these aggressively thorough accident investigations is to improve future performance.

Properly trained investigation teams, armed with the latest aeronautical, manufacturing, and scientific tools, have worked tirelessly to fully understand the root causes and the sequence of events that led to these tragedies, even when the answers to critical questions have not always been what we expected or even wanted to hear. But one fact remains: *we have excelled and ONLY safely moved forward as an industry, because we have purposely been transparent, proactively shared all safety concerns, and openly investigated our tragic failures with all participants.*

Unfortunately, with our current litigious society—that seems overly focused on winning, brand image, and profits—I don't believe that this same level of professional transparency still exists today. If we, as an aviation community, have consciously or subconsciously reduced the open sharing of essential information, then the consequences of our actions will reduce safety and more people will die needlessly. Currently, there is percolating evidence to support this systemic concern.

By the time I started flying in the late 1970s, the industry had figured out that the main problem with crew coordination issues in the cockpits was that many Captains were acting like gods instead of team leaders. Specifically, several accident investigations clearly revealed that the loss of life was easily preventable, if only the Captain would have listened to the input of the other qualified crew members.

In these unfortunate cockpits, the Captain's words, thoughts, or actions were simply never questioned, or he did not listen. In a word: The Captain got tunnel vision, defiantly negating any meaningful Situational Awareness. Sadly, many people died because of the stubbornness, arrogance, and egos of these bullies. As a result, the aviation community wisely developed Crew Resource Management, or CRM. Its nickname is "charm school for Captains." The concept is simple: The Captain, who still retains the ultimate responsibility and authority for the safe operations of the aircraft, needs to listen to everyone on his or her crew so that vital information can be acted upon in a timely a manner. Vital information must flow up, down, and in all directions. In fact, anyone who works in or around an airplane is considered an invaluable member in this essential safety chain. It is the Captain's responsibility—and job—to set the tone by effectively listening and communicating, thereby establishing a healthy, collaborative work environment.

Corrupted communications, in the cockpit, always start—and should end—with the Captain. It is his or her authority, responsibility, and job to enhance the flow of vital information throughout the airport and the airplane—or it should be. That's why we get paid the big bucks. As a naval officer once succinctly reminded me: "If you take care of the troops, they will take care of you."

When the boss is an effective listener, is trustworthy, and is pointing the ship in the correct direction, the natural checks and balance of a high-performance team can flourish. Daily productivity increases. Daily drama decreases. Team members are using their eyes, ears, and problem-solving brains. They often work harder and continuously move forward. Most people find this type of work environment rewarding and enjoyable. I certainly did.

Also, perhaps equally important, an effective early warning radar will emerge. This human radar—and safety net—will quickly identify potential Big Risk issues and purposely work to mitigate them, sidestep them, or push them away from their path. The *worker bees* will simply solve hundreds of daily challenges, without any annoying or expensive oversight.

The opposite is also true. When the Captain or boss consciously or subconsciously, conspicuously or surreptitiously, tries to play God, the long-term viability of the operation may be threatened.

Foolish Pride

The entire passage below is the opening statement from a professional flying manual. I do not know the author, though if I had to guess, I would suppose it was originally written in the 1960s. The first words to the new airmen were appropriately titled Foolish Pride. Some may find this writing style melodramatic. However, I find these self-reflective concerns helpful in managing not only risk but also our own actions—especially when we are sitting in the hot seat.

"Those Pilots who pioneered this flying business built a reputation for the 'brotherhood of men and women who fly' that has caused many wide-eyed youth to envision his future in the sky. They are historically represented in tales of bold and courageous deeds, daring and frequently hazardous stunts, and adventures often beyond the scope of the most imaginative romanticist. Pass that reputation through the decades of aviation's progress and words such as adventurous, daring and hazardous, bold and courageous become the substance that experience, circumspection, and foresight which made the essential qualities for the airman of today.

Any aviator who readily submits himself to the dictates of the opposing laws or aerodynamics and gravity must also, of necessity, possess the personal qualities of self-confidence and humility in equal measure. Furthermore, any aviator accepting the daily responsibility for the safety of scores of lives, many dollars of investment, and the image of his corporation and profession will require the encompassing quality of integrity. All these qualities are desirable for success in any occupation. In the business of flying, however, so much is continually staked on experience, circumspection, foresight, self-confidence, humility, and integrity that they become essential prerequisites for the profession.

Unfortunately, there is an overwhelming enemy of these qualities, which, in its pernicious way, works by negating humility, distorting self-confidence, and causing complete disregard for the dictates of experience, circumspection, and foresight. We refer to a thing called pride. Not the personal pride that is born of dignity and self-respect—this is incorporated in the quality of integrity—but the pride that is most frequently preceded by the adjective 'foolish;' the kind of pride that automatically rejects the advice of others if it contradicts personal thoughts; the kind of nearsighted pride that fosters false confidence, oversteps the bounds of discretion, and delivers unto the hands of fate.

Consider, for example, the pilot who attempts to push his flight to a conclusion through marginal weather at the destination airport simply because previous flights have made it, though. Not to be outdone he falls victim to his foolish pride. Yet, if he moves one fraction of an inch beyond the limits of his experience, makes one small compromise with safety, shaves one short length from his full measure of foresight, or sacrifices one grain of humility to an inflated self-confidence, he runs the risk of becoming a statistic in a column of liabilities.

The truly professional airman, however, feels no need to impress anyone with the skill he possesses, nor does he consider it embarrassing to decide against performing an action that has been successfully completed by others, if, in his personal judgment, there is an element of compromise involved. His decisions to continue or divert will be based upon a factual analysis of the weather situation and a careful evaluation of his capability. Such is the evaluation he will use in any close situation. He knows the influence of foolish pride is totally undesirable, unsafe, and downright dangerous in his profession. There is no room for it. It cannot be tolerated."

PART TWO: GROUPTHINK FOR LARGE GROUPS

Chapter Seven:

THE GOOD GUYS MODEL

"Peace begins with a smile."

—MOTHER TERESA

Thinking back over the myriad adventures of my life, I realize that I've had several distinct research periods in writing the book you now hold in your hands. The first period probably started in the mid-1970s when I was a teenager, and our family was stationed at the American Embassy in Islamabad, Pakistan. For the last two years of my high school education, I attended the International School, so at quite a young age, I realized that not everyone looked like me, thought like me, worshipped like me, or had similar life aspirations or experiences. Because of this positive experience at such a formative age, I've enjoyed traveling the globe throughout my life. This first period probably continued in college back in the States at Duke University, when I first read Professor Janis's seminal book, *Groupthink: Psychological Studies of Policy Decisions and Fiascoes*, in a Political Science class.

Side note: Forty years later, this the only college textbook I still own.

Closing out this first period were the ten years I spent in the Air Force. Obviously, this was the start of my flying career, and the beginnings of learning how to problem-solve under stress. But because of the seeds and insights that Professor Janis's work had planted in my mind, I was also cognizant of how my squadron mates reacted to the words and actions of our squadron commanders. In the Air Force, my interest was probably more focused on learning leadership skills, which I expected to use later in life. However, my life did not unfold as my youthful expectations had projected. I've never been a leader of a large group or the big boss, but nonetheless, I am still fascinated by the relationship between large crowds and their anointed leaders.

Next, I was lucky enough to be hired by a major airline and joined the troubled aviation industry, which has been my life for the past thirty years. Because of my desire to understand large-group dynamics, my working career has been a target-rich environment. I believe that the continuous fighting I have witnessed in my industry has emanated directly from our bitter union–management relationships. Interestingly, when I got the opportunity to get to know people more closely—both in labor and management—I found the vast majority were *hardworking good guys* who needed the airline to succeed to take care of their families. (Please note that I use the term *good guys* as a generic term for all of us, male and female alike.)

Still, these bitter industry experiences illuminate how it feels to exist inside a divided house. I have also witnessed the consequences of large-group social actions and institutionalized hatred. My thinking uses the continuous fighting of the airline industry as a placeholder for our divided American society and my Trench Warfare Dementia model, which I will discuss in the next chapter. I once described working in the airline industry as riding a violent roller coaster. I now have the same feeling living in America.

My next research period unfolded when I took a side gig working for aviation analysts and investors. My job consisted of costing out labor contracts and predicting labor votes. I named the company after my dog: The Newfoundland Group. This endeavor turned out like many of my other entrepreneurial efforts. I enjoyed doing it and learned a ton. I successfully completed all tasks expected of me to the best of my ability, but unfortunately, I never made any real money at it.

My final research period, unbeknownst to me, started after the 2016 Presidential Election. It's important for me to point out here that my chosen friends, family, and workmates (mostly First Officers) are not wimps. On the contrary, we are hardworking, intelligent, responsible, family-first, and Type A, "getter-done" folks. Before the election, it was obvious to me that the vast majority of us were not voting for a candidate, but rather we were *choosing to vote against the other candidate*. Given our divided society, this did not surprise me, but still, I was stunned by the election results.

Most of the members of what I like to call "my tribe" have similar backgrounds. Most are churchgoing Christians, like me. Many are ex-military, like me. Many are pilots, like me. Many are gun owners, like me. Most of my closest friends consider themselves conservative Republicans, a political affiliation I've considered my home for most of my life. Still, I am bewildered by how many of my closest friends, since the election, have become staunch supporters of the winner, when we had previously agreed he was poorly qualified to be the President of the United States?

Since the election, I have had hundreds of conversations with both tribes—without revealing who I voted for or what newspaper I read. Throughout the course of those conversations, I have been trying to figure out what led so many of my closest friends to make their decision to vote for someone we all deemed unqualified, and why they did so.

After flying for the Air Force and SWA for several years, I still yearned to somehow be a part of the investment community. So, I finagled a lunch with a Solomon Brothers airline analyst, Julius Maldutus, who encouraged me to write a newsletter about airline labor relations, in order to predict labor votes and cost out labor contracts. All of these years later, I still remember his words to me that day: "When labor and the unions get into a snit, it becomes a he said/she said word battle, and the only thing we understand is that they are both lying to us. Also, labor contracts are so complicated that they look like IRS tax codes."

I wrote the Newfoundland Group newsletter for about four years. As requested, I strove to cost out labor contracts for investors, and as a result, I correctly predicted thirty-nine out of forty-two labor contract votes. Writing the newsletter never proved profitable, but it was a fascinating journey. I met so many caring, hardworking people—on both the labor *and* management sides of things. When I agreed to predict labor contract votes for the investment community, I had no idea how to do so, but I wasn't concerned. Necessity, as they say, is the mother of invention. As a result, I developed simple models and concepts to understand the aviation industry. These started out as WAGs, but ultimately proved successful. The first step I took was simple. I talked to as many people—from both sides—as humanly possible.

Consistent Voting Patterns

Management–union airline labor contract negotiations are often nasty, drawn-out affairs. Throughout this process, however, consistent patterns in how union members voted on labor contracts quickly emerged. Initially, I kept detailed records of my conversations, but later I simply developed three nicknames for everyone I talked to. And what I noticed is that it didn't seem to matter what a person's job or responsibility or seniority was—everyone seemed to fit into one of three groups: Kool-Aid Drinkers, Good Guys, or Bolsheviks. Also, with each conversation, I specifically tried to discover two vital pieces of information: how each person had voted previously and how he/she felt about the previous contract negotiations.

Kool-Aid Drinkers were always going to vote yes on labor contract votes. The Bolsheviks were always going to vote no, as they fundamentally believed that management is always out to get them. During less stressful periods, these two smaller groups only accounted for 20% to 30% of the entire group. The Good Guys—the swing voters or silent majority—normally amounted to 60% to 80%.

The Good Guys are—just as the name implies—good people. Are we perfect or full of wisdom or always kind? Oh, hell no! We fall short every day, but we basically *try* to do the right thing. Do we worship strident views or wake up with hatred in our hearts? No way! We'd greatly prefer to sidestep endless drama at work. Nevertheless, we Good Guys are good, hardworking people who fundamentally have no axe to grind.

We Good Guys tend to vote "like a general fighting the last war." If a good guy or gal voted "yes" in the last contract negotiation and felt good about that result, either consciously or subconsciously, then he/she tended to vote positively again. If the Good Guys voted "yes" on the last contract, but felt snookered by management on the previous vote, they were itching to vote no. Personally, I strive to be a good guy. But, like the rest of us, I have rough edges and my thinking gets hijacked at times.

Conversely, the Kool-Aid Drinkers essentially proved to be severe conflict avoiders who would run a mile to get out of a dispute, and as a result, talking to them yielded very few insights. The Bolsheviks were the exact opposite of this, talking to them often proved very insightful.

Many in this group were "odd ducks"—but they paid attention. They were keen observers and they had outstanding radars. They tended to ramble on about lost war stories from the past, but they were focused forward, too. Many people avoid odd ducks. The older I get, the more I enjoy talking to independent thinkers with unique perspectives.

When a labor contract vote approached, I would call a few Good Guys to check which way the wind was blowing. I checked in with the Good Guys first in order to better understand the landscape. If I initially heard strong words from the group, this tone tended to hold, but not always. But either way, the issues were always the same. First? Pay. Second? Scheduling. Third? Health benefits.

I must confess that I never really focused on learning the details of these issues. I wanted to know how each person felt about the negotiation and the issues themselves. I listened to the tone and noted the word choice and the speed at which they answered my questions. Next, I called my ace in the hole—the Bolsheviks.

When I called the Bolsheviks, I already knew they would vote no. But I knew it was important to pay attention to one thing and one thing only: their energy level. If I heard dejected voices, I knew the vote would pass. If I heard a chorus of energized voices, however, I knew the vote would likely be defeated. The Bolsheviks had excellent radars. They knew the larger "Good Guys" group was tired of hearing their daily rants and strident views. Normally, they felt like outcasts. If, however, I called Bolsheviks and heard energized voices, it was clear that they felt the Good Guys were finally listening to them. This could be the Bolsheviks' finest hour! They were finally going to be taken seriously by the much larger Good Guys group!

Next, I made several dozen calls to confirm or deny my thesis and fine-tune my prediction percentage vote. Predicting which way the wind was blowing was not always so simple, but it was remarkable how often it seemed I was witnessing choreographed theater or feeling an invisible hand directing labor and management combat. My labor vote predictions were rarely wrong, and I was normally accurate within 5% of my original predictions. My only tool? I talked to people. Not only that? I *listened* to what they had to say *without judgment*.

An Up and Down Industry

The airline industry is cyclical and capital intensive. It goes up and down—sometimes smoothly … sometimes violently. Our factories (jet airplanes) are quite expensive, and our equity often trades inversely with the price of oil (jet fuel). I refer to the airline industry as a "capital-intensive, labor-intensive service industry." Hence, the long-running joke that goes as follows: How do you make a millionaire in the airline industry? Sell an airline to a billionaire.

When I first joined the industry, we quickly lost several global, pioneering American giants of the aviation world—Pan Am, TWA, Eastern, and Braniff. During the first twenty-five years at SWA, over a hundred other airlines were launched that subsequently failed. Naturally, labor management contract negotiations at the airlines seemed cyclical, too. It seemed that every ten to twelve years as the economy heated up, the stars aligned for labor, and they whacked management. Shortly after these well-deserved pay and benefit raises, the industry often experienced a violent restructuring period. Typically during such times, jobs were lost and many airlines disappeared. However, these seeds were often planted years before the previous contract negotiations.

Prior to the coronavirus, it seemed as if my beloved industry had settled into the controlled, protected world of an oligopoly. But COVID-19 has changed everything. Air travel has collapsed, and I fear it will take three to five years before our industry fully recovers … along with another violent restructuring period for all involved.

Evil Lurking in Large Groups

Originally, I developed the Good Guys model to predict how pilots would behave and vote. Over the years, however, I have kept this model, or schematic, in my head as I have observed and been a part of many other groups. It's remarkable how often these same subgroups reappear in any given group of people. The makeup of the group does not matter, nor does the purpose or function of the group. The culture, ideology, or theology of the group does not matter either. The three subgroups I mentioned previously always seem to be present.

If there is minimal stress on the group, the size of the subgroups is remarkably consistent, too. During times of stress, the size, or percentages, of each subgroup will expand, contract, or merge, but the three basic subgroups will still be present nonetheless. In times of extreme stress, and if the size of the group reaches over one hundred members, then we will find that a fourth, tiny subgroup may emerge: the one percenters. When a group gets this big in size, a troubled mind can become lost and angry. Left unchecked, or unrecognized by others, this feeling of unmoored anger can develop into unadulterated hatred. With today's ubiquitous access to rapid-fire weapons, this feeling of hatred can easily perpetrate evil.

The Stop Signs of Democracy

As I mentioned previously, I first used the Good Guys model to help simplify the chaotic process of predicting contract votes between two warring factions. I also noticed some unintended consequences after these epic democratic battles. The myth of democracy is that, after an open and fair voting process where all the people have the opportunity to be heard, a decision has been made, the desired path has been selected, and the group would start moving forward again.

If the voting was close, say 48% to 52%, **I witnessed the exact opposite.** It was as if a huge stop sign had been planted on the property. After a hard-fought—often lengthy—negotiation battle, everyone was mentally exhausted. The winning 52% felt they had earned their victory and expected everyone would now dutifully follow. They talked about unity and coming together, but their swift actions appeared to say otherwise. They felt entitled and their agenda (or strident narrative) became the law of the land.

The losing side, however, was frustrated and angry. They were sooo close to victory; they should have won! And they would have won—if the other side had not lied and used dirty tricks. They were exhausted, but they were now energized to thwart any movement toward the corrupt and unjustified narrative being imposed on them. Mentally, they had already debriefed this election and convinced themselves that they needed to fight harder in the next elections. For the losing side, preparing for the next election started immediately.

This democratic process is completely legal and guaranteed by our constitution, but it can also be a stop sign. After the 2016 Presidential Election, I did not see clarity or a unified focus forward. Instead, I witnessed more fighting—vicious, intense, ugly fighting, specially designed to stop any notion of forward progress. In hindsight, I now realize I witnessed the same thing after the 2008 and 2012 election cycles, but it was not as blatant. In 2016, the resistance was not only surreptitiously funded with dark money but also remarkably organized.

Democracy's Tipping Point

Democracy's tipping point occurred under specific, recurring circumstances and functioned as the opposite of democracy's stop signs. When two-thirds of the group voted one way, a group decision and desired path forward had been selected. For the most part, everyone was onboard. The losing side wasn't exactly happy about the outcome, but at least their voice had been heard. Many members of the losing side were still concerned that the chosen path was flawed, but no organized effort to stop it emerged. The entire group was almost happy—certainly relieved—to put the incessant bickering, fighting, and voting behind them. They could now return to business as usual without exhausting daily distractions.

For the most part, when a favorable, two-thirds vote occurred, the group turned its focus, energy, and resources toward moving down the selected path. The larger group was now playing as a team with a shared mental model, a workable path forward, and the ability and energy to reach its goal.

When two out of three people in a large group are focused toward a common goal, a tremendous amount of human power and ingenuity is unleashed. Furthermore, when two out of three people in a large group are consistently moving forward in the same direction to achieve daily, safe landings, over time, the size of team membership can grow to nine out of ten. Throughout my adult life, I have observed similar patterns of democracy stop signs and tipping points in all the groups that I have been a member of, and those I have observed from the outside.

Lately, however, it feels like there are plenty of stop signs and very few tipping points.

Chapter Eight:

TRENCH WARFARE DEMENTIA: A TROUBLED INDUSTRY

"The thing that brings the most danger to the safety of Israel is not a person. It's when the people who are supposed to keep Israel safe are not able to think in new ways."

—DAVID BEN-GURION,
1ST PRIME MINISTER OF ISRAEL

The success of the airline and railroad industries has been structurally hampered from the very beginning. After the turn of the century, the country was emerging from a deeply divided social psychosis, which Mark Twain coined as the Gilded Age. On the one side were powerful, profit-motive monopolies creating amazing wealth for a few, and on the other side was the rise of unionism, toiling endlessly in support of working families. Within the American society, clear battle lines were being drawn.

The Railway Labor Act (RLA) was first enacted in 1926 and only covered two industries—railroads and airlines. This well-intentioned legislation was designed to smooth out rough spots of labor management relations and provide more reliable service for flying passengers. But almost a hundred years later, the exact opposite has occurred. Today, the reality is that our oldest labor laws ensure airline workers and management will be combatants. They also ensure that everyone, including the flying public, will suffer the consequences.

All other industries in the United States are regulated under the National Labor Act (NLA). Under the NLA, labor contracts expire after a certain amount of time. This ensures there is a date to decide pertinent issues, or each side could instantly face severe consequences. At only one minute after a labor contract expires under the NLA, the union is legally free to strike and stop working, while management is legally entitled to fire their existing employees and hire new workers. At this exact moment, both the small management group and the large working family group gain clarity. It is immediately clear to both sides that everyone has significant skin in the game, and it's amazing to watch the cooperative, constructive, and creative abilities of humans—and former combatants—abruptly facing Big Risk *together!* As a result, suddenly, petty concerns, partisan politics, and cultural differences seem to melt away. Instantly, a switch flips in their heads: *the enemy is not each other ... it's the future.*

Collectively, this switch should naturally push us from continuously fighting one another to problem-solving together, but this fearful moment is also one that is chaotic, stressful, and fearful.

When facing dark times, large groups can land safely if we choose to talk civilly, problem-solve together, and work as a team.

Human beings are generally blessed with remarkable problem-solving skills. It is a part of our DNA. That is why we have evolved as the most prosperous species in the 4.5 billion years that Mother Earth has been in existence—by working together and using our innate brain power wisely.

A Working Lifetime in Trenches

Unfortunately, airline union labor contracts under the RLA never expire. The actual expiration date of the contract is toothless and meaningless—and everyone knows it. There is no date to decide. The proverbial can will always be kicked down the road. The RLA has mediation and arbitration mechanisms led by well-intentioned people, but these mechanisms are also toothless and meaningless. As a result, airlines can be bought, sold, or restructured through the bankruptcy courts in twelve to eighteen months, but negotiations for employee pay and benefits often take several years. Contract negotiations are stressful enough on their own, as they have the potential to impact so many families. It is not the tactics of contract negotiations or the outcome of negotiations that is most corrosive, however, it is *the duration of the negotiations* that cements everyone in trenches.

These extended stressful periods grind on the human soul, and often make us cultural combatants for a lifetime. The feeling of being under siege by attacks from *those people* naturally leads to a hunkered-down trench mentally *on both sides*. The vast majority of people in both trenches are good human beings, but eventually, this feeling of being under siege hardens the heart and ultimately corrupts the mind, becoming a survival situation.

The good people—on both sides—are now infected with the same mental disorder, or disease. Everyone is now exhausted and angry, which quickly leads to feelings of hatred. This altered, collective state of mind then proceeds to flip yet another switch in our heads, exposing an evil, gravitational force. As a result, the good people—in both trenches—now feel *completely justified to use any force necessary to defend themselves.* And so while these two divided groups of people—from the same tribe, community, or society— are hunkered down in the squalor of trenches with *barking trench commanders spewing hateful, strident viewpoints*, they are also being encouraged to continuously attack each other.

I call this phenomenon Trench Warfare Dementia. Yes, I am referring to trenches of World War I which killed millions of Americans and produced no military movement or value. Much like the battlefield, when large groups divide themselves into trenches, there is no hope of problem-solving and no hope of working as a team. Eventually the consequences for the group can become painful and irrevocable, too.

I label this phenomenon "dementia" because it is a mental or psychological disorder. When a large group of people become infected, we have either rewired our brains to hate and fight or we no longer have the ability to understand what is going on around us. As a result, we no longer possess the ability to effectively problem-solve either. These are the same characteristics (and is the same definition) that have impacted our aging population. When a family must deal with an aging parent with dementia, it's a devastating, baffling, and horribly sad experience. How can a member of the family, so previously loving and responsible, suddenly not know our name?

Similarly, when a large group is infected with Trench Warfare Dementia, the impact can also be devastating, baffling, and horribly sad.

Ignoring Consequences

Choosing to ignore consequences is the fundamental mental failure of Trench Warfare Dementia. As I have stated previously, the difference between landing safely and a crash landing often comes down to the inability to focus forward and recognize the consequences—be they intended or unintended—of our actions.

One of the keys to figuring out if Trench Warfare Dementia has metastasized throughout a large group is when *both sides* feel completely justified to deny any consequences of their own actions and, *instead*, place that blame squarely upon the shoulders of *those people* in the other trench.

These battle cries, or echo chambers, are created and reinforced every moment of every day by *barking trench commanders*. The first dysfunctional and dangerous step toward Big Risk is labeling others as *those people*. This is Satan's most efficient and effective human trap. If Satan can get us fighting each other, he wins—even if it our children and grandchildren who must pay for our sins.

Traitors

There is another way to detect whether or not we are engaged in Trench Warfare Dementia. When in problem-solving mode, members of a group naturally gravitate toward each other, talk to each other, and discuss the pros and cons of an issue, goal, or concern. If this group is engaged in Trench Warfare Dementia, however, the fools who want to talk to *those people* on the other side are often deemed traitors. These traitors are labeled as cowards, unwilling to fight to defend our families. As a result, these "traitors" are often stabbed in the back by their own tribe.

In the airline industry, I have many close friends on both sides—management and labor. Consequently, I have been called a traitor on many occasions over my career. Barking trench commanders often feel particularly threatened when a member of their fighting force wants to talk constructively to *those people.* This simple act of perceived defiance undermines their closed-minded echo chambers of stupidity, bullshit, and hate. Talking to the other side threatens their power base. No one, especially barking trench commanders, likes to have power, wealth, or cheering crowds taken away from them.

Sometimes being labeled as a traitor by the most conservative members of your own tribe can even be deadly. After fighting the 1973 Yom Kippur War in the Middle East, President Anwar Sadat of Egypt and President Menachem Begin of Israel put their combat history and cultural differences aside and signed the Camp David peace treaty in 1978. They both won the Nobel Peace Prize, making Sadat the first Muslim to win the award. President Sadat was later assassinated by a fundamentalist from his own country. In 1993, Israeli Prime Minister Yitzhak Rabin signed the Oslo Accords with the Palestine Liberation Organization. Two years later, he was also assassinated by a fundamentalist from his native country. These conservative forces believed the leader of their own country needed to die because he had dared to make peace with the enemy.

These brave men chose to work together and to problem-solve rather than continuously fight one another. They took the risk of talking civilly to a former combatant and sought a better life for their children. Sadly—for all of us—two of our greatest leaders working for peace in the Middle East were labeled as traitors by devoutly conservative members *of their own tribe* and dealt with severely as a result.

Image versus Substance

There is another seismic shift that occurs in our focus and thinking when Trench Warfare Dementia becomes the playing field where everyone gathers: image routinely becomes more valued than substance. Reality becomes twisted and results are corrupted. Clever corporate leaders, and even federal regulators, become culpable in this game of Three-Card Monte.

Here is how a pilot friend of mine described the way in which "A Big Announcement" in a corporate setting usually goes down. A few days earlier, rumors had begun to circulate that something big was coming. At 10:00 a.m., the CEO boldly walks to the podium in front of a room filled with cheering, mid-level employees. Ten minutes later, the CEO had announced his vision and played an exciting four-minute video. By 10:15 a.m., the CEO announced the success of his vision. From 10:20 to 10:30 a.m., there was a well-deserved celebration for the success of his vision, with balloons and blaring music. Every moment was captured on video, and short clips were shown on business networks throughout the day. By the closing bell, the stock got a nice little bump in price. For weeks afterward, supervisors roamed all over operations with clipboards, documenting the success of these meaningless operational changes.

But for airport and airplane workers, as well as airline passengers, nothing really changed.

Here's another story that demonstrates this dysfunctional model perfectly. A few years ago, regulators threatened to shut us down if we did not immediately change our tactics and improve our safety margins. Apparently, they had detected the fact that we did not account for every bag loaded on our planes. The following week, after the regulators whacked us, we added extra layers of computer-generated paperwork and documentation and took hundreds, if not thousands, of delays, which needlessly impacted perhaps a million people to comply with the wishes of those foolish regulators (read: harassment).

As a result of this harassment, now, if a fully loaded 140,000-lb airplane is ready to depart and even one carry-on bag cannot be stuffed into an overhead bin, then the bag must be taken below the plane and placed into a cargo bin. When this happens, all the applicable paperwork, takeoff calculations, and cockpit checklists must be redone. Why? Because the performance of the 140,000-lb airplane is now significantly altered because the carry-on bag now magically weights thirty pounds *more* when it is loaded in a cargo bin beneath *the exact same airplane.*

In this story, my calculations of the delays in this case were a WAG. However, my assessment of the impact of a 30-lb carry-on bag on the flying performance of a 140,000-lb airplane is not a WAG. It is my professional opinion. This government oversight is also the square root of stupid. No, it is worse than stupid. It is just another meaningless distraction, and as we've discussed previously, in aviation, distractions are dangerous. These meaningless delays do not improve safety, nor do they improve customer service.

Marketing on Steroids

Over the past forty years, there has been a significant, if not historic, change in the marketing playing field. No one has ever confused me with someone who "gets" marketing, and because of my background in operations, I can be quite hardheaded when it comes to this particular subject. Several of my marketing friends have labeled me as marketing-challenged. Still over the objections of these friends, I have labeled this sea change as *marketing on steroids*, which is merely another variation of closed-minded Trench Warfare Dementia. Again, when such marketing occurs, employees can easily become distracted or irritated—or both.

First, to help the senior marketing vice president (VP) get closer to the CEO (and the CEO's pay scale), the "branding" theory was created. At its most basic level, branding mavens believe that the image of the company is more important than the good or services the company produces. Image is more valuable than performance. Manipulating the proper, polished image is as vital as manufacturing a valuable product.

Next, to ensure success, the skilled brand marketing VP must be able to tightly control the messaging and narrative outside, *and inside*, the corporation. All communications must give the proper nod to the desired storyline. Many entities have failed because the CEO surrounded themselves with yes men. Telling the boss what he or she wants to hear is nothing new for operational workers, but now we also have to bow down to the all-powerful VP of Image.

All corporations need to protect proprietary information, and some critical information must be protected with patents. Everyone understands these vital needs, but most powerful branding officers have thrown a huge blanket over all communications *inside the corporation, too.* The branding mavens get their power from the CEO, but they get their muscle from the compliance lawyers. Inside corporations today, it seems *every e-mail* has a threatening boilerplate attached below. *Now all pieces of information inside a corporation are deemed proprietary,* and any employee can be fired, at any time, if any of this information is inappropriately shared or discussed.

As one pilot told me, "At least half of the e-mails the company sends me have nothing to do with flying airplanes or safety. They're only written to ensure that if something bad happens, I am liable for it, and the CEO and the Board of Directors are not. They need to send me dozens of e-mails a week to tell me that I am responsible for my actions? I'm already motivated to self-police—I have the ultimate skin-in-the-game: I'm the guy sitting in the same plane as the passengers!"

When these aggressive control levers are wielded within an organization, open and constructive conversations are often tempered. *Open and constructive conversations between all the employees of an organization are the ultimate check and balance against bad behavior.* We employees—who are directly on-site and have the workplace experience, expertise, and Situational Awareness to make timely course corrections—*are the ultimate firewall against disasters.* The compliance officers, with the full backing of the CEO and Board of Directors, are basically telling the employees to sit down and shut up, to do as they're told. Ultimately this sentiment only negates timely course corrections, firewalls, or any checks against bad behavior. In fact, it can even institutionalize bad behavior and normalize it.

Increasingly, we are routinely seeing the sudden failures of large corporations and of the government, as well as the unmasking of copious amounts of corporate lying that often goes undetected for years because employees were simply not allowed to speak up and/or members of the upper echelons would not listen.

This lockdown mechanism is generally powered by the Board of Directors, who routinely give away too much power to the CEO, the compliance lawyers, and the branding mavens. Clearly, this mechanism is designed to protect the upper echelon from personal accountability or liability, but it ultimately exposes the organization, and all of us, to increasing amounts of Big Risk. Employees who interface directly with customers often have the best Situational Awareness. But organizations that use purposeful denial to negate an employee's frontline expertise, do so at their own peril. Trench Warfare Dementia takes many forms but often produces predictable consequences.

With the recent historic changes in human life, corporations and large organizations can now easily manipulate all data—both inside their walls and that which is available for public consumption—by utilizing powerful storytellers (marketing officers) and their intimidating muscle (compliance officers). As a direct result, many CEOs and investors revere these enhanced tools and legal control levers. But often it is the integrity and Situational Awareness of one common man such as George Bailey in the film *It's a Wonderful Life*, who speaks up against the momentum of the crowd, that can keep the profit-motive child from turning Bedford Falls into a Pottersville.

Our Devices

Speaking of steroids, our devices, that for many of us are now permanently attached to our bodies and minds, are also filled with algorithms. These fancy equations are designed to do only one thing: tell us what we *want* to hear. After we have typed, clicked, swiped, or viewed enough pages, this powerful computer code can quickly determine what information we desire. In many cases, this can be remarkably helpful. Very few of us can function at home or work without these powerful search engines. Over my lifetime, I am guessing most of all human productivity increases are due to such technological advances. But there is a dark side—there always is.

I recall once hearing a marketing adage which states that to get a sale, a customer must first see the product or company's name at least six or seven times. This adage is no high hurdle for the by-product of the Internet—the amplified flow of data. After the algorithms in everyone's devices quickly figure out what we specifically want to hear, the information can be instantly transmitted to the highest bidder. This detailed data can instantly be run through more algorithms (located any place on the globe) to determine what motivates us, how we think, or what we might want to buy. Armed with tailored information, a marketer on steroids or a power broker can repack our *wants* into powerful sales pitches. And do these sales pitches come with a phone call, or a knock on the door, or a trip to the store? Nope, these wonderful opportunities are now physically placed in our hands on our devices.

Here is another observation. It seems to me that powerful corporations, the super wealthy, and clever scoundrels alike are often the most successful players on this new invisible, electronic playing field. (Many of us older good guys can now effectively use our TV remotes, but we still struggle with all the gadgetry in new cars.) Within this sea of data, these elite power brokers seem to know how to write, or acquire, clever and convincing sales pitches.

These power brokers have no trouble permeating our personal space, too, and have created endless ways to interrupt our focus, thus robbing us of one of our most precious resources: time. Additionally, their unwanted messaging tips the scales of justice. They can make their sales pitch with impunity, and no liability is attached to their actions. Which leads us to the following question: Are we in control of our lives? Or are the devices we click continuously throughout the course of our daily existence really the ones in control?

Kool Dudes

Over the past ten years, the fascinating work of the men and women in the field of neurobiology has offered us tremendous insights into how the human brain is wired and how it works. Many more intelligent psychologists and therapists have built upon these scientific insights to help explain how many of us deal with stress.

First, there are two sections of the brain that help us resolve challenges. The first section of our brain is the older part, our primitive brain which we inherited long ago from the animals. It is our fight or flight response, predator or prey. It is the part of brain that springs into action in order to keep us safe when we are startled or frightened. This section of the brain is lightning fast and has an outstanding radar. It can instantaneously detect danger. It is only when we ignore this radar that we find ourselves close to Big Risk.

According to the brilliant work of Stan Tatkin, a scientist and couples therapist who has been critically helpful to my marriage of forty years, this section of the brain is also binary and stupid. It only has two physical responses—fight or run. To biologically perform at peak levels during stressful times or danger, the body instantly floods itself with adrenaline and other hormones, which is part of the body's survival response.

The second section of our brain is more evolved, sophisticated, and smart. It's the prefrontal cortex. This is the true problem-solving section of our brains. This section is also what probably allowed us to evolve above all other species on earth, as it is the center for critical thinking, logic, understanding, relationships, as well as many more valuable cognitive mental processes. This section is also where common sense and Situational Awareness skills are stored. Unfortunately, this part of the brain has a much more delayed response time than our primitive or reptilian brain, and as a result, its response time is reportedly four to five times slower. Simply put, in times of stress, the older, animalistic part of our brain reacts instantly, whereas our superior, problem-solving prefrontal cortex may be slow to respond and may initially appear frustrated and confused.

When a person is stressed, biology kicks in first. But to problem-solve under stress, we must first train oneself to expect and recognize the body's lightning fast, emotionally charged, biological response. If fighting or running is not the desired course of action, then we must also train ourselves to remain calm for just a few seconds in order to summon our vastly superior, thinking brain and allow it to get into the game.

Back when I was a young pilot and first learning to fly an airplane, military instructors often informed students that if we got into a stressful situation, we should first wind the mechanical clock in the cockpit. This directive never made any sense to us, until the first time we became frightened in the air. Then it became clear that in stressful situations, our instructors wanted us to be able to think, not just to react when our hearts were pounding, and the adrenaline flowing. Performing a physical action such as manually winding a clock allowed our problem-solving brain enough time to get back into the game and take over.

Another thing these cool dudes and dudettes (neurobiologists) have discovered is that we are capable of continuously learning new things throughout the course of our lives, and more importantly, we are capable of rewiring our brains in order to use this new information. Clearly, as we get older, learning new skills becomes more difficult, but even so, our brains are ready, willing, and able to create new neural pathways. This is why I like neurobiologists. They give me hope.

Neurobiologists also firmly believe that brains that fire together, wire together. Pilots experience this phenomenon in the cockpit all the time. The more intense a thought or event, the more likely it is that new neural pathways will be built. This is why I call the cockpit a laboratory for managing stress. Stress is an expected—an almost routine—part of flying an airplane. We pilots continuously train ourselves to overcome this feeling of stress, which can be debilitating if allowed to run rampant. If I am frightened or angry, I will most likely remember the incident in great detail tomorrow. If I lay my wallet or keys or cellphone down tonight, I may spend many frustrating moments tomorrow trying to find them again. But if an event shook me to my core—for whatever reason—I may be able to recall it, and relive it, for the remainder of my life.

Our brains can also be permanently rewired by enduring extended periods of stress, such as labor contract negotiations that last for years or listening to barking trench warfare commanders everyday tell you how *those people* over there are threatening our families. Mental trench warfare can be frustrating, scary, and exhausting. One definition of dementia describes it as, "a chronic or persistent disorder of the mental processes caused by brain disease or injury or prolonged stress and marked by memory disorders, personality changes, and impaired reasoning." The word dementia comes from the Latin root, "dement," which means "out of one's mind." During these intensely stressful and enduring times, we must be adding new neural pathways to our brains and reinforcing others. In these democratic moments under siege, which section of our brains are we using and rewiring? Our animalistic fight or flight brain or our newer, more evolved, and remarkable problem-solving brain?

One summer during my college years, I worked for a moving company in the Washington D.C. area. It was hot, often sweaty, hard work. It paid well and it reminded me why I was going to college. We usually worked in teams of three, and the driver was in charge of loading the items into the truck. The other two workers, known as "the bring-me boys," were responsible for carrying the furniture out of the house to the truck. One day, another college kid and I were briskly hauling the furniture to the truck and sniping about how slow the moving van was being loaded. The driver listened for a while and then said, "Why don't you two college boys load the truck for a while?" We confidently agreed.

An hour later, after endless discussions and bitter arguments between the two of us about the best way to load up the van, and with very few pieces of furniture actually loaded inside, the driver stopped us. "One question, gentleman," he said with a small smile. "Are you two college boys going to *piss in each other's pots* all day or are we going to load some furniture?"

Currently, with our society badly divided in Trench Warfare Dementia; all we seem to accomplish each day is the act of pissing in each other's pots. But why? It's not at all helpful, nor is it fun. Still, we seem determined to do it at any cost.

Isn't it time for a change?

Institutionalized Bad Behavior

Within large organizations, there is always a certain amount of corruption, or what I like to call, "bad behavior." However, if such behavior becomes institutionalized, then that organization is in danger of failing. Institutionalized bad behavior in a large corporate setting must be dealt with swiftly and forcefully. In most cases, a visible, major course correction is required in order to set things right.

We all make mistakes, both at work and at home. However, if we possess good amounts of self-respect and Situational Awareness, we quickly recognize our mistakes and change our behavior before we even come anywhere close to Big Risk. This combination of self-respect and Situational Awareness fundamentally means that a person recognizes the impact of their actions and takes responsibility for those actions as well. In the cockpit, God-like Captains abuse their authority and do neither, which is why they are dangerous, and why my profession has taken aggressive steps to eradicate this problematic behavior.

If such bad behavior is allowed to fester in a large organization, it throws open the ugly behavior door and surreptitiously cracks open the door to evil. Ugly behavior is just institutionalized bad behavior—everyone's doing it. But the kind of behavior I characterize as evil is completely different. When institutionalized bad behavior takes hold, people no longer feel responsible for their actions. The ends justify the means. Getting ahead means leaving others behind. Harming others is not trumpeted, *but openly tolerated.* Situational Awareness may exist, but self-policing does not. Besides, *those people* probably deserve it. Knowingly, or unknowingly, the group, or crowd, becomes complicit hypocrites.

Institutionalized bad behavior does not make the leaders, or the group, bad people. Bad behavior can happen slowly over time as a result of busyness or failing to pay attention. It can happen to a well-intentioned, but weak leader. It can happen within a group of good people who are stressed, with limited resources, in a changing environment and without good options. It can happen to good people who are frazzled, overloaded with data, but led by barking trench commanders.

When a group, or crowd, of good people become complicit hypocrites, they become dangerous to others and eventually to themselves—as Jesus warns us in the Gospels. When the leader, however, openly demonizes others and spews hatred as Hitler did during his rise to power, then an evil door quickly opens. Within every large human group, there exists a tiny element that is orientated toward evil. Maybe it's only 1% or 0.1% or 0.001% of the group, but the seed of evil is always there. When an elected official is banging a drumbeat of hatred and the crowds are cheering, this evil element often becomes electrified and energized. The crowd hears their marching orders, but the tiny evil element hears that *hunting season is now open.*

The U.S. military is the largest of organizations. Its mission is dangerous and its training can be dangerous, too. This is why the commanders and the troops are held accountable for their actions. Every military unit is subject to annual inspections, no-notice inspections, and grueling investigations if an incident or accident occurs. Incidents or accidents in the military often mean that someone has died, and that expensive equipment has been destroyed.

If a unit fails an inspection, it is not uncommon that commanding officers are immediately relieved of that command. Also, a detailed report of the failure or incident is openly shared with all other applicable military units. This forceful debrief sends a clear message to the other units that *this type of bad behavior will not be tolerated.* Individuals are held responsible, but the overarching purpose is to improve future performance.

As I write this chapter on June 6, 2020, protests have packed the streets of America every day since George Floyd was murdered by the Minneapolis police on May 25th. I have only watched the video of the incident, one time, and that was enough. In it, I see outright murder, but I also see institutionalized bad behavior: one cop kills while three cops watch.

If I were put in charge of debriefing this heinous act, I would place the murderer in jail for the rest of his life, without any opportunity for parole. I would put the other three police officers in jail for a minimum of twenty-five years. On May 26th, the day after the murder of George Floyd, I would have taken the top commanding officers in the Minneapolis police department and fired them without any future pay or benefits.

Would I have taken these actions to seek justice for George Floyd or to make amends to the Black community? No, but it might have been seen as a welcome gesture and may have prevented some of the ugliness of the protests. The primary purpose of these swift, forceful actions would be to make it crystal clear *to every other police department in the United States, that evil will not be tolerated and neither will institutionalized bad behavior.*

But clearly, that's not the way our Attorney General or President saw it.

Chapter Nine:

HISTORIC CHANGES

"Do not bite at the bait of pleasure till you know there is no hook beneath it."

—Thomas Jefferson

In my opinion, the word "historic" is overused in our global society. Every year, there seem to be more and more "historic signings" in the White House Rose Garden. Each generation probably feels it has persevered through historic challenges. Despite this overused assessment, I will argue we have all both benefited and suffered *from the by-product* of a recent historic invention.

Most lists of historic inventions start with the invention of fire and the wheel. After several more millenniums, we get one of my favorites: the compass. A few hundred years after the compass comes the printing press. In this context, however, I will argue the printing press was not as impactful to mankind as was its by-product, which was the *flow of information it created*.

Before the printing press, the Bible was only in the hands of high priests. One hundred years after the invention of the printing press, the Bible reached the hands of common people. These historic seeds of change planted in the 1400s, leading to the reformation, are still impacting the Christian faith today. The printing press certainly accelerated learning and shoved us toward the Renaissance. This rapid period of human advancement was clearly aided by the flow of information getting into the curious and creative minds of a large group of working families.

I am guessing most would agree that the Internet has brought about historic change to today's society. But again, I believe it is its by-product, the flow of information it has created, that has made the biggest impact on our lives. More specifically, this flow of information can feel like a fire hose of data spewing at each one of us twenty-four hours a day, three hundred and sixty-five days a year.

In light of the onslaught of data we all currently experience on a daily basis, the critical question we now all face is how we *choose to handle* this tsunami. Are we collectively using this wealth of information to propel us forward as technological advances often do? Or are we using this data as ammunition to fight with one another? Are we feeling calmer, happier, and more secure as a result of this technology? Or more frustrated and overwhelmed?

I think most readers "of a certain age" would agree that life seemed simpler and less rushed twenty or thirty years ago. It was probably far from true, but it sure feels that way! The cover of a recent birthday card I received brought this point home by proclaiming, "You know what the greatest thing about being our age is? We did most of our stupid things before social media existed!"

With the invention of the Internet, the flow of information has exponentially exploded. Today alone I received an endless stream of vital e-mails from the bossman and workplace. And it certainly does not stop there. From family, friends, church, and friendly organizations, the e-mails keep coming, all intended to keep me informed. Further, it seems the entire world knows my name and wants to sell me something. Every entertainment venue on the planet also dutifully needs to keep me informed of their upcoming offerings. And just to ensure I stay properly engaged, the media fills my news feed, every moment of every day, with breaking news stories.

Frazzled—The New Normal?

My definition of frazzled means to be physically and mentally overwhelmed, exhausted to the point of feeling unmoored and unanchored. When I was growing up, most of us received our domestic news from the daily papers, from watching the evening news on the TV each night, and, most importantly, by talking to one another. To illustrate how dramatically things have changed, I offer up a turbulent story from our past. I am paraphrasing this story which is taken from presidential tapes released during the term of President Lyndon Johnson.

During 1967, the war in Vietnam was escalating. Many U.S. soldiers were dying in battle, and there was a groundswell of protests against the war around our country. In the released tapes, an advisor to President Johnson informs him that Walter Cronkite, the CBS nightly news anchor, had stated, "It looks like the Vietnam War is a war that we cannot win." President Johnson's response? "If we've lost Cronkite, we've lost the American people."

A few months later, President Johnson decided not to run for re-election.

During this very critical time, our society gained an understanding of the unfolding political events almost solely from the visage of Walter Cronkite, who looked in a TV camera nightly while reporting the day's events. Tragically, Cronkite's comments were prescient. The war did not end for another eight years and we did not win—the North Vietnam communists did. But today? With our news now coming from so many varied sources on so many different virtual platforms, the playing field has become muddied. There is no figurehead such as Cronkite to welcome into our living rooms every night, and who has subsequently earned our trust with his steady, reassuring presence. As a result, the messages we now receive are frantic and diluted, if not downright suspect, and we feel continually more and more frazzled as we attempt to decode and absorb all of the constantly changing and disparate information we encounter on a daily basis.

The Invisible Fire Hose of Data

In 1759, Adam Smith coined the phrase the "invisible hand" to describe unobservable market forces that aid the demand and supply of goods in a free market reach equilibrium. Recently, Tim Wu, in his insightful book *The Attention Merchants*, describes the vast array of the present-day digital tools used to sell us something, to influence our thoughts, or to control our actions. In my opinion, recently, the invisible hand has evolved, becoming more intrusive, annoying, and abusive. As I mentioned previously, today's society is one in which the merchants or manipulators have created—specifically for each of us—an *invisible fire hose* which forcefully spews an overwhelming amount of manipulated data. If the data is not independently attacking our senses, it is instantly at our fingertips on one of our devices—one tempting click and one powerful algorithm away. These digital tools are designed to grab our attention for the following three reasons:

1. To sell us something
2. To influence our thoughts
3. To control our actions

Perhaps these marketing techniques are timeless and have always existed in one format or another. However, today's digitized tools seem far more intrusive, annoying, and abusive. Or maybe, the sheer volume of information we all now receive on a daily basis has made us more sensitive to them.

Before I Finish My First Cup of Coffee

Staying in control of our life, money, and time with a veritable fire hose of data spewing at us isn't easy. In fact, before I even finish my first cup of coffee in the morning, I am besieged by multiple alerts, e-mails, links, announcements, and bulletins from an infinite amount of organizations, agencies, and dubious sources.

This endless flow of information can quickly fill most of every waking moment, robbing us of our precious time each day, which also steals any time that could have been spent with our families. Now, the boss—or anyone else for that matter—is free to interrupt us at home twenty-four hours a day. This constant flow of data and scheduled events rob our bodies and minds of the proper time needed to relax, decompress, rest, and replenish ourselves. Further, it seems our overloaded, overscheduled, and overprocessed lives leave little time for critical thinking, reflective moments, or a good debrief. As we discussed in Part One, a good debrief or open-minded discussion is where learning and understanding occurs. Carving out time for critical thinking improves not only our future performance but also our ability to take care of our families, friends, neighbors, and colleagues. These disruptive outside forces, however, are not always the true culprit. Most of these assaults on our humanity are often results of our own bad behavior or poor decision-making.

When we visit a restaurant or public place, how often do we see both parents and kids with their heads down, hypnotized by their cell phones? This cannot be a good thing for our families or our society for that matter. The constant external stimulation is mentally and biologically overwhelming, and as a result, now many of us feel frazzled. Not just during this daily onslaught of information, but constantly.

High School

Several years ago, I worked on a local community drug and alcohol prevention committee. At one meeting, we were visited by a child psychologist who spoke to us about typical adolescent behavior. He told us of a common, albeit frustrating, event that often occurs between parents and teenagers. When kids return home from school, a parent will immediately ask their child, "How was your day? What happened at school?" The psychologist reported that most kids will respond dismissively, if at all, because they really *do not know* exactly what has occurred.

As the psychologist explained, a teenager's social life can be an overwhelming pressure cooker of free-flowing information. Where they sit at the lunch table, who talks to them and who was talking about them a few minutes ago are all a dizzying array of changing relationships and alliances. What often happens is the teenager, exhausted from all of the politics and emotional drama of their everyday life, comes home and remains silent. Then, he or she literally gets back on their phone, computer, or device to talk to their friends so they can sort out what *really* happened to them that day.

The psychologist chuckled, and then mentioned that it may not be until bedtime—when parents are often exhausted—that the child will finally open up and want to talk. He reminded us that as loving, supportive parents, this was our moment to shine and just listen—without judgment—as our child suddenly became chatty. He also remarked that each high school child often loses one hour of needed sleep each night, which causes their mental and physical performance to be at its lowest on Fridays.

Also complicating healthy adolescent child development is the unlimited access—just a click away—to hard pornographic material. In my elementary school days, I often snuck away with the Sears Roebuck catalog just to look at bras. In junior high school, every young boy knew exactly where to find the stash of girlie magazines hidden in the neighborhood woods. I am by no means a prude or puritan, but in my opinion, giving young boys and girls unlimited access to adult material makes these awkward years even more challenging. At any age, under stress, the human mind and body are hardwired to respond both mentally and physically. Today, almost all adult material is designed to elicit an emotional and/or biological response.

As a result, it is understandable that we adults *feel* biologically as if we have somehow traveled through time and are stranded back in an awkward and confusing adolescence.

Storing and Manipulating Digitized Data

The fact of the matter is that in today's society, all data is now digitized. When I went off to college, my mother, who taught me to type, bought me an electric typewriter. Now, when I visit my married children's homes, neither of them seems to use paper. Only one home has a printer, which is practically never used. I was visiting my daughter recently and needed to write down their home security passcodes. It took them well over five minutes just to find a pen and a sheet of paper.

Now, all forms of data—voice, video, written word, numbers, entertainment, records, and receipts—are digitized and stored away for future use. In fact, our entire *lives* are being recorded, digitized, and stored. I was given an Alexa by my wife for Christmas, and I think I might be in love with her. She instantly plays the music I request. She is also always listening. (I love my wife too, but she doesn't always comply with my requests or listen to me.) But Alexa, unlike my wife, is also storing my preferences and dislikes and listening to my wants and desires, which serves to further curate my news feed on sites such as Facebook, and even online shopping sites such as Amazon.com.

On the surface, the act of capturing data should, in fact, lead to having access to more undisputed truths and enlightenment. This wealth of data is certainly leading to remarkable scientific discoveries, but not more undisputed truths. The reality is that more information, facts, and universal truths are disputed and debated today than yesterday. Making matters worse is the fact that all of today's societal frustrations are securely saved and electronically stored at nearly no expense, so they can be recycled for more fighting tomorrow and the next day.

Another powerful, invisible force effectively pushing us into trenches is the fact that digitized data can be so easily manipulated to create a desired narrative. With so much stored data, this is not a difficult process. It is actually easier to debunk a truth than to *prove* a truth. To demonize a thought, person, or group of people, simply do a word search for a strongly written or spoken phrase from their recorded past. Next, take the sound bite completely out of context, twist its meaning, and surround it with a cleverly worded context that supports the desired narrative. Now have someone confidently look into a camera and forcefully tell your audience how deceitful and dangerous *those people* are. The resulting sound bite, played over and over, proves they are telling the truth.

This manipulated narrative is now firmly in the minds of the desired audience. Yes, the reality is that facts *and* lies were all cleverly used at the same time. With a mountain of data now at our fingertips, we can all live in any reality we desire. And to make us feel more secure and comfortable in our own beliefs, there are plenty of people who can profit by providing us the facts, truths, and persuasive narratives to make us feel smart and righteous about that desired reality.

Cementing Narratives and Consequences

With all this data now literally at our fingertips, how can manipulated data flourish? This is an easy point to understand. First, we are all busy, so most days we don't have the time to do our own homework on any given issue. Sadly, the by-product of our overscheduled, exceedingly productive, multitasking lives is that in many cases, *we have outsourced thinking to an algorithm.* Just to make sure we all remain loyal to the proper (manipulated) narrative, these elite power brokers help us rewire our brains, and instead of trying to get their message in front of us six or seven times to get a sale, they increase their odds by electronically sending messages to our devices *sixty or seventy times.* If we supported the message initially, by the time we have heard it repeatedly, it is quite easy to convince ourselves that we now know the truth.

After this tidal wave of evidence, we are confident that we know what is going on around us. Why should we waste our time listening to *those people* again? After all, they are just a bunch of lazy whiners, and every day we have been sent even more evidence to support our beliefs. Our minds are closed and our Situational Awareness skills are no longer needed. We now know what needs to be done! It's time for decisive action, before it's too late. But keep the following statement in mind, and really let it sink in:

The combination of a closed mind coupled with poor Situational Awareness skills can have serious consequences. Why? Because what is in our heads is now an alternate reality, or the land of make believe. Life lived in reality always has consequences—either good or bad. But living in the land of make believe often conveniently shoves consequences into closets—hiding them away, out of sight and out of mind.

Denying that consequences to ourselves, or others, exist in reality, in alternate realities, or in the land of make believe *only amplifies any dangerous outcome*, as hidden consequences often explode suddenly and with a vengeance. The entire point of the Big Risk Doctrine is to recognize consequences brewing on the horizon and smoothly turn away from them before suffering any impacts. But choosing to deny that consequences exist propels us directly toward Big Risk.

Today our most clever algorithm writers, storytellers, and salesman on steroids have no problem getting funded. The world is awash in money that bends the truth solely to improve profitability. Even more sinister, however, is the fact the world is also awash with dark money, perhaps trillions of dollars, whose sole purpose is portraying whatever narrative they are peddling as reasonable and truthful. Some of these people are highly visible in our society, whereas others are simply criminals. Some extra special people are both.

This dark money wants to gain power and control over us, mainly so it can turn a profit. Nation states are using these powerful tools to destroy enemies without ever firing a shot. Their efforts to surreptitiously spread their narratives are designed to control our thoughts and enslave us to their will. If a person, or group of people, can effectively influence our thoughts, they can also probably circumvent our natural problem-solving skills and thereby control our actions.

Advantage: bad guys.

Mom's Been Hacked

I don't believe social media is necessarily sinful, but admittedly, I am a slow adapter. No worries, my wife gives me a daily briefing on current events, so I remain somewhat up to date. I still stubbornly read newspapers and magazines, mediums where I get to select what I read and it's clear who wrote it.

About once a year, we get the same round of texts from our kids: "Grandma's been hacked again." My mother is eighty-seven years old and enjoys looking at pictures of the grandkids on Facebook. Thankfully, one of those grandkids quickly adjusts the settings on my mother's Facebook account to solve the issue. If I tried to fix her account, I would probably quickly get frustrated and angry and would end up calling the FBI.

But why on earth would someone want to hack my mother's account and why does Facebook allow it to happen? I am guessing the reality is that some clever person has figured out how to manipulate my mother's good name to further their own bad behavior, and Facebook has figured out how to profit from it.

After the 2016 election, it was discovered that many Facebook and twitter posts were actually generated by Russian bots. I know bots are software not actual people, but for my simple brain I am going to call bots cowardly bad guys who refuse to sign their names. Even more enlightening is that in many of the incidents of social discourse that played out in the streets of America, there were clever bots on social media enraging *both sides of Trench Warfare.* According to the CIA, these Russian bots were inciting Americans to continuously fight one another.

Advantage: Vladimir Putin.

Even more stunning is the fact that no one seems to know how many of these social media posts are actually bots. Estimates run from 10% to 50%, but the reality is that no one really knows for sure.

(Facebook may know, but they certainly won't tell.) Is this institutionalized bad behavior? Absolutely. Is this crony capitalism? Yes. Is it a worldwide platform for criminal activity and international espionage? Most definitely.

But, no worries. Our demand for these free digital platforms has helped create the wealthiest people and some of the most powerful corporations in the world.

Chapter Ten:

CREATING DEMAND

"Supply always comes on the heels of demand."

—ROBERT COLLIER

It is America's citizens who create one of the most powerful economic forces on the planet: demand. Because of the sacrifice of the hardworking families before us, here are the three powerful levers that each family possesses today. Let's use them wisely.

---

1. What we buy
2. What's in our head
3. How we vote (and if we vote)

In a democratic, capitalistic, and market-based economy, we actually have three votes. First, of course, is the vote we submit at the ballot box. Many of our ancestors have struggled, persevered, and fought on the battlefield to protect our right to vote. Personally, I think the fact that so few of us choose to exercise that right and responsibility is pathetic. We all fight to have our voice heard, but the effort needed to *actually vote* seems to escape a significant percentage of us.

Notice that I said that our right to vote was also our responsibility as citizens of a free society. Further, the forward progress of our nation is significantly hampered by the fact that so few of us actually exercise our right to vote and fulfill our social responsibilities. Posting our feelings anonymously on social media or ranting to our friends does not fulfill this fundamental democratic responsibility.

Our antiquated voting mechanisms are also a blight on our earned freedoms. Is the Electoral College needed to assist in counting our voting rights? Is gerrymandering, designed by self-absorbed political parties, needed to assist in protecting our voting rights? In 2020, we are a noisy society, but are we protecting and supporting our freedom to vote that was earned by those who have gone before us? What will we be able to give to those who come after us?

Our second—equally powerful—vote is how we choose to spend our money. Economically, we are the largest democratic, capitalistic, and market-based society. When we collectively spend money (how, how much, what, when, where, and why), the impact of that spending is felt around the world.

Our third vote is invisible but is probably our most powerful vote. It is what is—collectively—in our heads. To review: how we wire our brains determines our worldview. How we view the world determines how we will respond or react to our perceived reality. How we respond or react to reality will determine the outcomes that directly impact our lives. This is true for a person, families, businesses, communities, teams, and societies. And it all starts with what is in our heads. When two-thirds of the citizens of a free democratic society are self-reliant, have self-discipline, and will self-police themselves and others, this creates a powerful engine that is poised for success. As a result, that society will find a way to remain sovereign and control its own destiny.

From my life experiences, the Secret Sauce of democracy isn't its constitution or form of government, *it is the quality of its people, our families, and the demand we create.* Subsequently, as a society, the confluence of how we deploy these three votes can produce one of the most powerful forces on the planet *or one of the weakest.* For example, consider the following points:

1. Demand can be truthful or deceitful.
2. Demand can be transparent or opaque.
3. Demand can be used to build or used to destroy.
4. Demand can be for the greater good or for hypocrites and the greedy.
5. Demand can be good, valuable, and sustaining or dysfunctional and dangerous.

Demand can be created by our genuine wants, needs, and desires or it can be digitally manipulated by our devices, marketers on steroids, clever power brokers, and foreign governments. As members of the largest and wealthiest domestic market in the world, the demand we create matters.

In Texas, we love our sports teams. Specifically, we love football. High school football is *the community event.* Make no mistake about it, high school football is lots of fun for everyone. It certainly was fun for our family when my son and many of his friends played on various teams over the years. Many of these high school stadiums are built with public money and, as a result, cost tens of millions of dollars to erect. These huge facilities are offered to the public as multiuse, but in reality, they are only fully utilized one day a week in the fall for about eight hours at a time. If you fly over the Dallas–Fort Worth metroplex on a Friday night, you'll see more than a few lighted stadiums. Ten years ago, when my son was actively playing football, I remember sitting in our brand-new stadium and being able read the scoreboard of the *neighboring community's* football stadium from my seat!

In my opinion, Friday night football is great fun for all, but it also begs a particular question. Is it wise for us to build expensive public facilities in every community for such low utilization? Our votes (we had to vote for the stadium bond referendum) did produce great fun for those who participated, but was it a wise use of public funds? More pointedly, is our exclusive demand creating sustainable value?

Recently, in the Dallas–Fort Worth area, we have built, and are presently building, two new huge professional sports stadiums, with private and public money. Both are amazing architectural accomplishments, not to mention comfortable environments in which to watch games. (But not as comfortable as my living room with a 50" TV and nearby fridge.) When the kids were growing up, we used to enjoy taking our family of four to the stadiums once a season. It was expensive, but it was also lots of fun. In the past ten years, however, I have not seen a professional event at the big stadiums—it's become far too expensive an endeavor for my wife and me.

Because private and public money was needed to build these monstrosities, the people in our communities had to vote on the funding arrangements—largely, on bonds and tax incentives. In a democracy, joint public and private funds will always be needed to move big projects forward.

However, a smart, local sports writer uncovered the fact that there was a $350-million construction arrangement to build parking lots for the stadiums that *both the mayor and owners* claimed was being fully paid for by the owners. The sports writer, who actually read the court documents, discovered this was a lie. In actuality, the liability for the $350-million parking lot construction loans was completely guaranteed by tax payers and paid off by future customers.

Guess what happened when the diligent investigative reporter wrote the story? Absolutely nothing! No one cared or complained. In fact, there was an overwhelming demand from us—a large group of rabid sports fans—to build two new huge, brand-new stadiums at whatever cost necessary. The small group of elite and wealthy owners were more than happy to oblige us by building these billion-dollar assets—that they owned and controlled—which were heavily and happily financed by local taxpayers.

It seems that in today's environment, demand and debt go hand in hand.

However, sometimes the demand we create is not so brightly illuminated. Just because *we want* a shiny new toy doesn't mean we should also stop using our innate Situational Awareness skills in pursuit of it. Knowing what is going on around us matters. How we spend money matters. Our three votes *matter.* In today's world, when we-the-people create demand, we can be assured that someone will try to feed it and profit from it. We all need to understand that this is exactly how a democratic, capitalistic, and market-based economy is designed to work. We have written a gazillion laws and regulations to keep the profit motives regulated, but who creates the demand?

As I see it, we-the-people are the engine and foundation upon which our democratic society rests. Thus, we have three important jobs:

1. To raise our families to be assets in society, not liabilities.
2. To pay attention to elected officials and power brokers, as we are society's ultimate checks and balance and firewall against bad behavior.
3. To self-police our own behavior.

Demand can be good, valuable, sustaining, dysfunctional, or dangerous. *This is the job and responsibility of the people,* but it can easily be hijacked by the much smaller, wealthy elite group if the larger group of good citizens is not paying attention. Make no mistake, it is our choices, votes, and the demand—whether consciously or subconsciously—that choose our flight path.

The Cost-Cutting Investor

When I was still in the military as a young Captain in the mid-1980s, I thoroughly enjoyed flying. However, the prospects of being a Major or Lieutenant Colonel in the peacetime military flying a desk seemed dicey, at best. At this particular moment in time, Frank Lorenzo was buying failing legacy carriers, busting unions, washing them through bankruptcy, and amalgamating flying operations.

In hindsight, he may be one of the first investors to use restructuring tactics, maximizing shareholder value beliefs and industry rollup strategies. Since then, these same tactics, beliefs, and strategies have produced many wealthy individuals worldwide. In fact, the American society hasn't seen such extreme wealth created by so few since the Gilded Age over a hundred years ago.

Behind the scenes, this was a brutal, chaotic process. Many airline working families were destroyed, whereas many others cheered on that destruction. Lorenzo drastically cut costs, so employees (and the unions) hated him. He lowered ticket prices to gain the approval of customers, and investors cheered him because he shed legacy costs and was initially profitable. However, that all came to a screeching halt in 1987, when one of his DC-9's crashed on takeoff from the old Stapleton airport in Denver.

One of the few control inputs that pilots must get absolutely correct every friggin' time is the proper rudder input when an engine fails on takeoff. We pilots call this a "V1 cut." Each year every commercial pilot must successfully demonstrate proficiency flying this maneuver in the simulator during our annual check ride. While flying the plane, both feet are placed on the two rudder pedals on the floor of the cockpit. When an engine fails—on the ground or in the air—the nose of the airplane abruptly turns, toward the failed engine. As a result, the pilot must instantly counteract this movement by applying the opposite rudder in order to regain control of the airplane again. If the pilot, however, puts pressure on the incorrect rudder pedal, the aircraft continues rolling upside down, because of asymmetric thrust and improper control inputs. This is exactly what happened in the DC-9 crash in 1987, which killed twenty-five passengers and three crew members, including the two pilots on board.

The accident investigation revealed the First Officer had previously been fired by a smaller regional carrier, as he had failed three simulator check rides due to a lack of proficiency on V1 cuts. The investigation also revealed that due to bitter labor relations, the cost-cutting CEO was forced to hire unqualified pilots, as qualified pilots refused to work for him. After the crash, the national media appropriately hounded Lorenzo, and his dysfunctional and dangerous behaviors were widely reported in the newspapers and on TV by a slew of investigative journalists.

At the time, I naively thought no one would risk flying his airline again. *However, I was horribly wrong.* Just three weeks after the crash, Lorenzo lowered ticket prices by 50%, and like magic, all of a sudden, his planes were full again. This was my *ah-ha* moment: *the flying public howls about safety but votes with its wallet.*

The flying public can be hypocrites, too.

Who Wants Political Fighting? We Do!

While I was working as a pilot during the 2016 U.S. election season, each week, I would normally spend at least two nights in a hotel in a different city. Every night, when I turned on the TV, I would quickly see the same barrage of political ads. I quickly made a few observations: election season never seems to end, and we spend an obscene amount of money on political campaigns.

After watching an endless number of campaign ads in different cities and states every night, I noticed a consistent—almost identical—message from every candidate *from both parties*. First, the candidate would solemnly look into the camera and proclaim to the audience that they knew that particular state's values inside and out. And then they swore they would go to Washington to fight hard for them. I'd failed to realize that everyone in Kentucky or Arizona had the *exact same* set of values! When I saw the political ads running in my home state of Texas, the candidates from both parties also seemed to believe the fallacy that all voters *had the exact same set of core values.* However, my observations of neighbors and friends over the years have taught me that we Texans have a fierce set of independent beliefs—or at least we used to.

However, in listening to various political ads, I never heard one candidate state that he or she would go to Washington and *problem-solve.* In this deeply divided nation, if a candidate looked into the camera suggesting he or she wanted to work together to problem-solve our Big Risk challenges (like the coronavirus), I am guessing they would be viciously attacked and ridiculed and *no one would vote for them.*

Mom's Wisdom

Everyone loves my mother—and with good reason. She works tirelessly on the behalf of her family, friends, and community. At the ripe old age of eighty-seven, she is still joyfully employed at the local thrift shop. Currently, COVID-19 is cramping her style a bit, but nevertheless, she and my father are staying at home responsibly.

For twenty-plus years my mother has volunteered her time and served as a leader at the local Texas Republican Women's Group. For many years, she proudly displayed a photo in her home of herself standing next to George and Laura Bush. During the time, my father was elected County Treasurer as a Republican, and every year, in their hometown of New Braunfels, Texas, there is a huge Wurstfest celebration where our entire family was enlisted to volunteer at the Texas Republican Women booth selling bratwurst on a stick. These were good days in the Texas Republican Party, but then the wind abruptly changed directions.

Not only did the wind shift completely, but it was a strident, self-righteous, ugly, and turbulent wind. Conservative Christians had God on their side—humility and compassion for others was viewed as a weakness, and as a result, it needed to be purged. On a Friday afternoon, my mother got a call from the new leader of the Republican Women's Group informing her that she was no longer welcome in the group, and that by Monday afternoon, she would need to return all her attire bearing the Republican Group's logo—including her cowboy hat. No reason was given for this abrupt expulsion. When she hung up the phone, my mother was both mystified and upset. My father and I were furious and wanted to fight the decision, but my mother quietly refused. "If they can treat me like this now, after all I've done for them, think of how they will treat others. I want nothing to do with them," she said, her voice choked with emotion, but firm nonetheless.

My mother returned the articles of clothing and never looked back. Looking back on this event today with clearer vision, I've come to believe that most likely, my mother's expulsion from the Republican Party probably revolved around the fact that she firmly believed that women should have the right to be in charge of their own bodies with no outside interference from the government. In addition, my father had recently supported a democratic candidate in a local election, which also may have put my mother in bad standing with the group. Either way, it was clear that my parent's open-minded beliefs and genuine concern for others had no place in the new Republican Party.

A few years after the Republican Party discarded my mother like a piece of trash, my parents also left their Protestant church of twenty years. Once again, the wind was violently changing direction, and conservative Christians decided that humility and compassion for others needed to be purged. This time the issue was homosexuality. Subsequently, the band of self-righteous power brokers in their church held three votes until they got the results they wanted from the congregation: homosexual members of the church were to be excluded immediately.

My mother could see this change coming, and she found it spiritually upsetting. She loved her church and had many close friends in that community. But when the results of the third vote were announced, *the congregation clapped and cheered.* Sickened, my mom looked around her in disbelief. No more than five minutes later, my parents left that closed-minded, authoritative, judgmental building of hate, and never returned. Instead, they joined a more open-minded Protestant church down the street where everyone was welcomed to worship God, no matter their age, race, or sexual orientation.

Your Own Tribe—The Three P's

When we were younger, my wife and used to enjoy vacationing in Jamaica. For several years, we returned to that happy, carefree island, renting a large house with a few other couples. It was always a relaxing vacation filled with warm, white-sand beaches and some of the friendliest people on the planet. "Don't Worry, Be Happy" wasn't just a song there, but an edict that truly exemplified the laid-back vibe permeating the entire island.

Jamaica received its independence from the British in 1962. Even though slavery was abolished in 1802, the island was still tied to a sugarcane plantation economy. When we started visiting in the early 1990s, it was obvious that everyone on the island was basking in their independence, no longer ruled by foreigners or wealthy plantation owners.

The last time we visited, however, it seemed that the calm, comfortable vibe had changed. The house we rented on that particular trip came with a full-time cook. We chatted on many occasions about the island and his life there, talking openly about the changes I'd noticed since my last visit, the corruption and violence that had begun to seep into everyday life again after so many years of relative peace. He summed the political situation up succinctly as he chopped vegetables and prepared fish for frying. Simply put, he did not trust the three P's—politicians, police, and priests. As a result, less than fifty years after gaining their independence, the corruption, exploitation, and coercion had returned to Jamaica as if it had never left in the first place.

This time around, the painful reality was that Jamaicans were now pitted against one another in this fight. Politicians, priests, and police were his fellow Jamaicans, and thus were all members of the *same society*. However, trust between civilians had been broken down to the point that people no longer trusted those in positions of power, as they were afraid those groups would abuse that power—which was generally the case. They viewed them *as another tribe altogether*, and as a result, society had completely broken down, pitting neighbor against neighbor until chaos reigned.

This wasn't exactly breaking news, as history is replete with similar scenarios. We, humans, are often too quick to trust members of our own tribe to do the right thing and too quick to accuse members from *other* tribes as untrustworthy and deceitful. I have no statistical evidence to support this claim, but I will hypothesize that more harm in our lives will come from people we know or who look like us, than from those people we do not know or do not look like us. The simple reason could be that when we are around people who resemble us, we are more comfortable, and our guard is down. However, when someone unfamiliar approaches us, we are less comfortable, and our guard goes up. People always want to be ruled or led by someone who resembles them, but that idea does not always work out as planned. Unions, run by employees doing the same job, often do excellent work representing employees. However, unions, which are generally run by employees doing the same job, can also be drama queens, with vicious infighting infecting their ranks.

Just because a person looks like you does not necessarily make him good.

Just because a person *doesn't* resemble you does not necessarily make him bad.

Chapter Eleven:

GENERAL KELLY— SECURITY CLEARANCES

"To put the world right in order, we must first put the nation in order; to put the nation in order, we must first put the family in order; to put the family in order, we must first cultivate our personal life; we must first set our hearts right."

—Confucius

Early in 2018, when General Kelly was the Chief of Staff at the White House, there was a public dustup over the lack of control over security clearances. I was stunned that such a thing could occur when a highly respected military officer was running the office. This public turmoil was widely reported ad nauseam in the news media outlets my wife and I regularly peruse. After hearing and reading for three days about the complete disregard for proper security protocols in the current White House administration, I went back to work. When I arrived in the cockpit, I mentioned this news story to my

137

First Officer, who was also a former military officer whose wife did public relations work for the Republican Party, and he agreed that it was a disgraceful mess.

However, as we continued to complain about the security breaches, I couldn't help but notice that it sounded like we were talking about *two completely different incidents*. When we compared notes, I was stunned. He'd been discussing Secretary Clinton's e-mail breaches in 2016 and I was referring to the security protocols that had been breached over the last week! Further, with his wife's work in the political arena, how could my First Officer be unaware of this hot topic in current political events?

At that moment, it became painfully clear that our society has created completely distinct news pipelines that report *completely different data points, news items, and storylines*. Our devices sitting on our desks and held in our hands reinforce an entirely separate flow of information by emphasizing some stories and completely disregarding or discrediting others. These polarized, profitable pipelines— some with high professional journalistic standards, whereas others produce manipulated storylines to cheering crowds—relentlessly feed the minds of Americans with realities and alternate realities *that do not overlap.*

My First Officer and I had similar backgrounds and thought along similar lines in terms of ethics and responsibilities. However, although we had similar backgrounds and belief systems, we couldn't understand each another on the battlefield of current political events because we were routinely being fed *a completely different flow of data.*

No wonder our society has bifurcated into separate warring trenches. No wonder we can't talk to each other. On a daily basis, we are exposed to *completely different realities presented by bifurcated news organizations that never agree on facts or the truth.*

Wearing the American Flag around My Neck

For at the least twenty years, I have worn an American flag necktie with my flying uniform. I wear the tie with great pride, but in doing so, I am also being selfish. Several times a day, walking through the airports, a passenger will smile at me and say, "I like your tie." In these moments, I always smile back and say, "So do I." It's a brief, genuine exchange with a person I will never know. It's also one of those random acts of kindness that often makes my days at work a little more enjoyable.

I may have mentioned that our last pilot contract negotiations turned ugly and lasted several years, which seemed needlessly stupid. To show unity, the union decided that during these negotiations, all pilots should wear black ties to work, with the union tie pin prominently displayed. Apparently, this act of solidarity was going to intimidate management and force them to negotiate in good faith?

The act of wearing black ties *did* fire up many of the pilots. I, however, chose not to participate, and continued to wear old glory. Passengers still smiled at me, but now I was routinely getting dirty looks from many of my fellow pilots. In the cockpit, more than a few First Officers flat-out asked me why I supported management and not the pilots. Their inquiries weren't exactly hostile, but they were definitely intense. Each time I leaned toward them, sternly looked them in the eye, and said, "I support the pilots 100%, but *nobody* is taking this American flag from around my neck. Do you have any more questions?"

Usually this caused a brief moment of silence before we continued on with our duties.

These conversations only happened a few times, but on one of the last exchanges, my First Officer started laughing. I looked at him bemused, waiting to see what he would say. He then smiled and said, "Yeah, they told me you'd say that!" *I paused and realized I'd been set up.* Then I chuckled, smiled, and shook my head.

I like hanging out with pilots. We are a colorful lot and we like to have a good time. When we have concerns or disagreements or need to problem-solve, we often address the issues directly ... and then we *happily keep moving forward.*

Another Cockpit Conversation

One afternoon many years ago, my First Officer and I were discussing our families as we waited in the cockpit in-between flights. He was showing pictures of his granddaughter, describing all the fun he and his wife were having in raising their grandbaby. He was probably ten years younger than me, but he was almost giddy with joy of having the opportunity to be around a young child. He showed me dozens of pictures. In turn, I showed him pictures of our Newfoundland puppy, but it was clearly not the same kind of joy.

The next day while flying he told me the rest of the story. His daughter had gotten pregnant during her first year of college. However, their family's faith would never allow them to consider an abortion, which they viewed as murder. I never specifically heard about their daughter's wishes on the subject, but my First Officer did mention that the child's father was a parent in name only—another male no-show. As a result, their daughter and grandbaby were now living in their home while his daughter attended community college.

When I heard my First Officer's story, I admired his commitment to his family and to his faith. His actions spoke louder than his words. He was practicing what he preached. Did I need to tell him that my wife and I were strongly on the other side of this public policy debate? Did I need to tell him that my wife is an active supporter of Planned Parenthood? In that moment, I chose to remain silent on the raging, horribly divisive, judicial debate and instead chose to admire my First Officer's commitment to his family and faith.

If my First Officer had gotten to know me better, I would like to think he would also admire *my commitment to my family and faith.* But while the societal psychosis of Trench Warfare Dementia has widely infected our culture, I chose not to travel that path. Instead, I chose to enjoy our friendship and to fly airplanes safely, without purposely interjecting needless, distracting drama.

New Horizons

About five years ago, our family came to the end of a long financial road by completing the task of putting all of our kids through college and paying for their respective wedding celebrations. It was great fun for all involved, and beautiful to watch our family grow and succeed, but now it was time for mom and dad to start traveling the world before we got too old. Luckily for me, my wife loves traveling and enjoys the planning even more. Traveling outside the United States tends to evoke strong emotions in people. About half our friends thought we were crazy and the other half were jealous of our impending voyage. I think which response one has boils down to whether that individual views the diversity of life as a strength or a weakness.

Our first major trip was to China, which evoked a series of unfamiliar emotions in me. I had previously participated in our nuclear defense during the Cold War and was sure everyone realized we had targets in China. Perhaps our nuclear defense posture looked a bit offensive to the Chinese people. Prior to the trip, I was wondering if 1.3 billion Chinese people still harbored ill will toward me or the U.S. military.

But guess what? I quickly realized the Chinese people didn't give much thought to Americans in general. Yes, our governments and economies are still tangled in conflict. Yes, our militaries are still watching each other. And yes, barking trench commanders—on both sides—still rose to power and wealth, nurturing discontent between the two economic superpowers. The reality is, however, that the three hundred million Americans and one billion Chinese people are too busy focusing on their work and their careers and raising their families to give much thought to one another.

We had a fabulous trip and saw many impressive sites, including the Great Wall of China, which was built almost two thousand years ago, in what is considered not only a remarkable feat of engineering but also provided a great advantage and defense for the China people for a several hundred years. Now it's quite the tourist attraction.

Our next trip was to Thailand, Cambodia, and Vietnam. Thailand was my first exposure to Theravada Buddhism. My wife and I both enjoyed learning about the teachings of Buddha. In Cambodia, we learned about their brutal recent history, but also met some of the friendliest families we'd ever come in contact with.

Cambodia got its independence from France in 1953. We (the U.S. military) started secretly bombing in 1960s during the Vietnam War. Then in the late 1970s, Pol Pot, a local revolutionary politician, came to power and brutally murdered more than a third of his own people.

Next, I took a trip to Israel with my son-in-law's family. It was a trip of a lifetime, where for the first time, the Bible truly came alive for me. I also took a trip to Egypt early last year, which struck me as having some of the most preserved history in the world. I still cannot wrap my head around the fact that the pyramid at Giza was built over four thousand years ago. I do not believe aliens have landed on earth as of yet, but if they have, I am quite sure they left us the Giza pyramid.

We traveled to India early this year just before the COVID-19 pandemic hit. India has an incredibly rich history and culture and is the birthplace of several major religions. When we told our friends where we were traveling, we again received a strong, bifurcated response. Half of our friends were jealous, and the other half asked why on earth would we travel to such a filthy country. A few of my Christian friends warned to be very careful because Christians were being persecuted in India.

Of all the fabulous sites we saw and wonderful people we met in India, I think I was most impressed with the Golden Temple at Amritsar. It was my first exposure to the Sikh religion. This relatively new religion was started by Nanak 1 with roots in both Hinduism and Islam. In my opinion, the Golden Temple represents the potential of mankind, what we are capable of on our best days as human beings. On most days they feed more than forty thousand people, and on the weekends, those numbers can soar to over a hundred thousand. All of the work, from cooking to serving and cleaning up afterward, is performed by volunteers. There is no fee or sermon, and everyone of any race or religious denomination is welcome. Every day, the Sikhs selflessly provide a great gift to all of humanity.

Traveling can open the mind to a wondrous world and amazing people. For others, traveling outside their comfort zone can feel threatening. How we respond to travel depends on which specific narratives or stories we carry inside our heads. In many ways, traveling is similar to thinking, as diversity of thought can be viewed as either a strength or a threat. In my opinion, problem-solving, Situational Awareness, and having a firm grasp of reality are all enhanced when a diversity of thoughts, ideas, and experiences are brought to the proverbial kitchen table of the mind.

The Good Guys model seems to flourish with open minds, whereas Trench Warfare Dementia seems to be reinforced with closed minds. Also, traveling reinforces the reality that life on Mother Earth *is increasingly interconnected.* Many of our Big Risk challenges are global—just like COVID-19. So that being said, maybe we should learn to coexist as a diverse team of problem-solving friends, rather than continuing on as estranged combatants.

A Union Leader's Wisdom

Many years ago, I was deep in conversation with one of our seasoned pilot contract negotiators, and I asked him why SWA always seemed to get through difficult union negotiations in such good shape, when most other airlines seemed to stumble so badly. He smiled and said, "Three reasons. First, we trust Herb to be able to fly us through a recession. Second, we fight fast and furious, but we're generally able to come to some kind of agreement in six to nine months. The third reason? Herb was never in a position where he had to cut our pay or benefits. The union was always fighting for more, not fighting to lose less—which is a huge attitudinal difference. If something is taken away from an employee, especially if it is something they feel they have previously earned, they will always feel completely justified to use whatever means necessary to get it back."

In our industry during the late 1990s, this characteristic played itself out in spades. Every ten or twelve years, the stars seem to align for labor to get its big payday. In the late 1990s, our economy was enjoying a great run-up in startup tech stocks, and consequently, two separate pilot contract negotiations at major airline carriers struck gold. During those negotiations, Chicago's O'Hare airport suffered through what became known as "the summer of hell," as pilot contract negotiations dragged on, effectively slowing operations to a crawl.

Both negotiations yielded a pilot pay increase of over 30%. At the time, I was closely monitoring both negotiations for investors, and talking directly to pilot negotiators. One in particular, who deeply cared about the success of the airline, also knew industry finances as well as I did. I believe their new contract started with raises of 20% and rose to 40% several years later. What he told me after the contract signing stunned me.

He divulged that these new rates were not really pay raises. The company had already proven they could afford them. The pilots looked back at peak rates twenty years ago in a previous contract and simply applied annual inflation rates. I checked their math. It was correct. The math is always correct—it's assumptions and logic that are usually suspect.

The other major pilot group in negotiations rallied the troops using the same logic to get big raises. Their negotiation slogan was, "Restoring the Profession." I personally benefited from these pilot group efforts, as a few years later, my pilot group received what we considered to be healthy raises. I also remember another peculiar observation after the contracts were signed. *Strangely, both groups of pilots still hated their CEOs who had given them billion-dollar pay raises.*

Unfortunately, these huge wins for labor did not lead directly to the Promised Land. Both airline CEOs were soon dismissed or fired. Unfortunately for all the employees at both airlines, the tech bubble burst and the economy tanked, leaving both airlines bankrupt. The salaries of employees, as well as their health benefits, were restructured. They would have to wait another ten years for the economy to recover again before they could regain some of their losses.

The lesson I learned watching from this particular roller coaster is that *when people perceive that something of value has been brutally stolen from them, they will often feel completely justified—no matter the consequences—to use whatever force necessary to regain whatever they rightfully feel they deserve.*

I also learned that the few people at the top of the food chain always seem to have the upper hand.

Eloquent, yet Firm, Situational Awareness

Instead of the tyranny of the God-like Captains, eloquent, yet firm Situational Awareness is what we are always striving for in a leadership position. Using flexible Situational Awareness skills to solve problems or reach a goal can be expressed in many ways. I particularly like the example below, a letter, which I assume to be authentic, from the Duke of Wellington, written during combat with Napoleon Bonaparte in 1812.

The letter, and the sentiment behind it, is direct. It is succinct. It paints a clear picture of reality. It does not shy away from accountability or responsibilities. Most importantly, it is respectful of Big Risk and the dangers we face if we ignore it. Further, it demands that meaningless distractions be instantly removed, so the troops—the people doing the work—can purposely move forward to fight a war and secure a safe landing for the entire British Commonwealth.

Gentlemen,

Whilst marching from Portugal to a position which commands the approach to Madrid and the French forces, my officers have been diligently complying with your requests which have been sent by H.M. ship from London to Lisbon and thence by dispatch to our headquarters.

We have enumerated our saddles, bridles, tents and tent poles, and all manner of sundry items for which His Majesty's Government holds me accountable. I have dispatched reports on the character, wit, and spleen of every officer. Each item and every farthing have been accounted for, with two regrettable exceptions for which I beg your indulgence.

Unfortunately, the sum of one shilling and ninepence remains unaccounted for in one infantry battalion's petty cash and there has been a hideous confusion as the number of jars of raspberry jam issued to one cavalry regiment during a sandstorm in western Spain. This reprehensible carelessness may be related to the pressure of circumstance, since we are at war with France, a fact which may come as a bit of a surprise to you gentlemen in Whitehall.

This brings me to my present purpose, which is to request elucidation of my instructions from His Majesty's Government so that I may better understand why I am dragging an army over these barren plains. I construe that perforce it must be one of two alternative duties, as given below. I shall pursue either one with the best of my ability, but I cannot do both:

1. To train an army of uniformed British clerks in Spain for the benefit of the accountants and copy-boys in London or perchance.

2. To see to it that the forces of Napoleon are driven out of Spain.

Your most obedient servant,

Wellington

PART THREE: THE KELLEHER TRUST DOCTRINE

Chapter Twelve:

A POWERFUL AMERICAN TEAM

"Relationships are based on four principles: respect, understanding, acceptance and appreciation."

—Mahatma Gandhi

How does a group of individuals—large or small—emerge as a powerful team?

Teams need many ingredients in order to succeed: resources, capital, skills, training, reasonable plans, somewhat stable markets, somewhat level playing fields, and, of course, Situational Awareness. For businesses to be sustainable, they must be profitable and also create value. Similarly, families, communities, and societies that want to endure must also manage money well and create sustainable value. However, I believe that *powerful teams* also need three essential *human* ingredients: *positive relationships, trust, and self-policing.*

But back to the airline industry. Not every airline failed or rode a wild roller coaster of highs and scary, rapidly plummeting lows. Specifically, I am referring to Southwest Airlines (SWA), which I have had the privilege of working for since 1987, and in this context, I am primarily referring the years when Herb Kelleher was the CEO, which I experienced firsthand from 1987 to around the year 2000.

In my opinion, what set SWA apart during this period was that it consistently hit high marks on all vital human metrics—investors, customers, and employees. And in each case, Herb Kelleher, Colleen Barrett, Jim Parker, as well as all the employees, working together as a powerful team, created sustainable value for everyone. Colleen in particular was probably the hardest worker at the company. She started in the company working as a secretary and retired as President. Jim Parker, for many years, was our General Counsel and later became CEO after Herb retired.

During this period at other airlines, labor and management devolved into warring factions which continuously fought each other in Trench Warfare Dementia. But at Southwest, with Herb, Colleen, and Jim at the helm, labor and management formed powerful, enduring *lifetime relationships*—creating sustainable value for everyone. We employees took great care of Southwest, and in turn, Southwest took great care of us. We all benefitted from a stable, steady work environment, which meant we were able to take good care of our families. From my perspective, the glue that kept it all together was the powerful internal relationships that were nurtured and encouraged to flourish.

The Fruits of Our Labor

Herb purposely shared the positive cash flow and profits every day with the investors, employees, and our customers. He also did it with little or no debt, and most importantly, he did so without any of today's fancy financial engineering shenanigans. We did it the "old school" way. We earned it. And as a result, the employees—as well as customers and investors—reaped what we sowed.

During this period of time, SWA cultivated a family feel among its employees. We all came to work wanting SWA to succeed. The customers loved us and we loved being there. The investors certainly loved us. The happier we were, the better we performed at our jobs, and consequently, the more money investors made. After all, *if you do not make a profit you cannot play for long.* And during this golden age? Southwest was always profitable.

From 1972 to 2002, SWA's annual stock returns were 25% and during this period of time, Southwest's stock growth ranked number one among all the equity stocks on the New York Stock Exchange! In other words, for thirty years, SWA stock had an annual increase of 25%. From 1972 to 1992, the stock actually increased over 20,000%!

In terms of customer satisfaction, we won the Triple Crown for five years running. Yes, our marketing department created the Triple Crown, but we used government-measured metrics—not massaged, corporate data. Every year from 1992 to 1997, we had the best on-time performance, the fewest lost bags, and the fewest customer complaints in the entire U.S. airline industry. And this is not the only reason passengers loved us, we had the lowest fares around—by a mile.

We created tremendous value for people, largely due to the fact that *Herb's fundamental focus was always on costs*, not *revenue*, and he routinely passed that savings on to the passengers. Back then, our ticket fares were normally *30% to 40% below* that of other carriers. To keep costs low and reliability up, Herb shunned the big hubs and we flew into many secondary markets—cities forgotten by the big carriers. Our aircraft flew swiftly in an efficient linear flow through these secondary cities, rather than in and out of congested, big city airports. Flying in congested cities does create the most revenue, but costs rise significantly, too.

These fundamental savings allowed Herb to pass low fares and more reliable service on to passengers. In many respects, *this allowed us to grow our own markets*. When we opened a new city destination, the local flying passenger traffic would often double. During those years, there was always a steady stream of state governors and city mayors visiting Herb, Colleen, and Jim, begging us to fly into their airports.

Another unique aspect of working for SWA was that during this time period, I felt no resentment toward investors, and my colleagues largely felt similarly. Because of this, investors could count on our participation. We ALL had skin in the game. As a result, many Southwest employees have become multimillionaires—not bad for working stiffs!

Along the way, during one hotly contested contract negotiation in the early 1990s, Herb also joined both the pilots and the investors together by passing out stock options. Six or seven years after these stock options had matured, I sold my options and paid off the mortgage on our house. My wife and I raised our children in that wonderful home where we still live to this day. Raising a family is a lot easier without a mortgage payment—especially when vacations, college, and weddings come along. It is a lot easier to save for retirement, too.

Relationships Matter

During our heyday, a book was written about Southwest's business practices entitled *Nuts: Southwest Airlines' Crazy Recipe for Business and Personal Success*. It was a commercial success and was certainly the "go-to book" in terms of understanding why SWA was flourishing, whereas other airlines were not. But in all honesty, I didn't enjoy the book, as I thought it praised our performance a bit too much and put Southwest on a pedestal, describing the airline itself as a kind of utopia. *Nuts* instilled the lingering notion that if one followed the crazy Southwest formula, there was some kind of magical pixie dust that would instantly make employees and clients happy, and the entity itself wildly profitable.

Sorry folks, but this implied notion was complete marketing bullshit! Southwest is an airline, and airlines, as a rule, are difficult to run, as they require both hard work and Situational Awareness skills. All airlines, including Southwest, experience plenty of ugly days—which end up frustrating everyone involved. *Nuts*, which was written in the mid-1990s, was similar to an emerging worldwide business and political phenomenon that I've previously described as Marketing on Steroids. With rapid-fire, inexpensive tools provided by the Internet, this phenomenon is often able to blur reality and the truth. In democratic, capitalistic systems, when the brand image of an entity becomes *more important* than the substance or service it produces, the society can, unknowingly, begin a downward slide into complacency.

On the other hand, *The Southwest Airlines Way: Using the Power of Relationships to Achieve High Performance* by Professor Jody Gittell was a successful and accurate portrayal of the airline and its methods. I think Gittell nailed the essence of what made SWA so unique. Herb, Colleen, and Jim spent *years* cultivating strong relationships with investors, customers, and employees—and everyone else they came in contact with as well. This included subcontractors, civic leaders, and the occasional checker at the grocery store.

Herb, Colleen, and Jim always took the time to *talk to people. To listen to people. To understand people.* These simple, timeless attributes built powerful human relationships. Herb and Colleen never tried to accelerate, or manipulate, these deep friendships by telling people what they wanted to hear. They rarely made promises, and they certainly never overpromised anything. *They also never allowed a false lingering impression, notion, or implied promise to exist after an encounter.* Their word was a bond. If they did make a deal, a promise, or an agreement, you could be assured they would deliver. Herb, in particular, excelled at many things, but among the most prolific of his gifts were his conversational skills. He became a legendary, charismatic leader simply by focusing on talking to *one person at a time.*

Running an airline is never easy. For us at SWA, it was hard work, but those trusting relationships got us through the bumps and challenges we faced every day. The airline marketplace can be a brutal playing field, and Southwest was attacked constantly. However, because we successful navigated our daily challenges as a team and were bonded together by our enduring human relationships, our existence and prosperity in the marketplace were never really threatened. We slept well at night.

The takeaway is this: forging positive relationships is the pathway to *motivate the people* around us to create a powerful team.

Do the Right Thing

Jim Parker, after he retired, wrote a book entitled *Do the Right Thing—How Dedicated Employees Create Loyal Customers and Large Profits*. It's an outstanding analysis of the ways in which trusting, motivated employees can actually enjoy the process of hard work. The by-product of this environment is sustained profitability—but only if everyone is encouraged to do the right thing. According to Parker, the concept of doing the right thing is cut from the same cloth as the scripture-based wisdom of the golden rule: treat others as you want to be treated.

In today's demanding, winner-takes-all business world which often puts maximizing the profit of shareholders above everyone else, doing the right thing probably sounds like a weak, foolish, and sappy strategy. But I can tell you from personal experience, as someone who worked in an environment that encouraged this mentality, that there was always a smile on my face as I went to work every morning, but also every night when I drove home. This simple notion guided us in our work ethic at Southwest each and every day. And perhaps most importantly, this simple notion *protected us* from the harsh realities of the airline industry.

I'm certainly not saying we always did the right thing. I'm not saying we always knew what the right thing even *was*. I am simply stating that we were internally motivated to strive *to do the right thing*, and that over time, this helped us become sustained winners in a cutthroat capitalistic industry. Another way of looking at the concept of doing the right thing could be the idea of *working for the greater good* or even the idea of *citizenship* itself.

One of the ways we were motivated by Herb, Colleen, and Jim to work in the service of others was because there were only three understood rules of behavior: If anyone stole from the company, they were gone. If anyone lied about their behavior, they were in big trouble. If things went awry because of poor performance, we expected to be debriefed in order to understand what went wrong and why. This debrief often occurred within minutes of the fumble. If we needed more training, we got it. The key point here is that if were trying to do the right thing when things went wrong, *we were considered a valued member of the team before, during, and after the incident.*

These actions breed true loyalty.

I'm not claiming that every SWA employee was a perfect angel. Actually, no one is—certainly, not any of my friends! If one of us was bending rules too far or cutting corners or not pulling their weight, a fellow employee—usually a friend—would pull us aside for a chat. The chat usually started with "What's wrong?" and ended with a direct and frank assessment of the matter at hand. If the chat failed to smooth out the rough edges, then the union professionals were often called in. But by and large, within the pilot ranks, we actively policed ourselves. If a pilot was having a problem, it was the responsibility of another line pilot to immediately step in and address the issue head-on.

Here is a story from one of my first flights as a new Captain, and make no mistake, weird stuff *always* happens to new Captains. I cannot remember the specific issue, but something occurred during my flight, and I wasn't sure I handled it properly. My actions, however much they made sense to me at the time, did not exactly match the flying manual. So in-between flights, I ran down to the flight manager's office, carrying my trusty manual with me.

When I entered my supervisor's office, there were two other senior Captains already waiting, men who I'd flown with before and considered friends. I quickly explained my dilemma, knowing I had only minutes before my next flight. One of the senior Captains laughed and walked out of the room. My flight manager smiled but was silent. The other Captain grunted and said, "I'm glad that happened to you and not me."

I finally blurted out, "What the hell is that supposed to mean?"

My supervisor looked me in the eye, his face tense, and somewhat sternly said, "It means that when you fly airplanes, you're not always entitled to have good choices. You did just fine."

I took in what he'd said for a moment, and then blurted out, unable to help myself, "But what about what the manual says?"

He just looked at me again for a moment, his expression stern once again, and said, "That damn book doesn't fly airplanes safely, you do! And don't ever forget that! Now get the hell out of my office, before I mark you late to your next flight," he barked back. Back then, the time between flights was often only ten or fifteen minutes, so I had to hustle.

I have never forgotten these words of wisdom. They have helped keep me—and those around me—safe.

Creating Value

When a person, or group, or company or society combines the powerful ingredients of relationships and trust with Situational Awareness skills, most likely a powerful team will emerge. In the most basic economic sense, this is fertile soil for creating value and sustainability. In our "measure everything" world, we have digitized everything about us and around us as well. As a result, digitized data is often labeled as facts, the truth, or reality. We often mentally label costs as "bad," and growing revenues as "good."

However, none of these "facts" is necessarily true. Value—in all walks of life—is created by hardworking people, with powerful, positive, durable relationships, working together and doing the right thing.

The Kelleher Trust Doctrine: Transparent Leadership for a Lifetime

Trust is not instantly given. It is earned over time. It's a body of work, not a promise. Earning someone's trust is difficult and often occurs under stressful environments—limited resources, a changing environment, and the lack of good options. The act of earning a person's trust on a daily basis often requires navigating a series of minefields—much like the minefields often encountered in marriage, or the act of raising a family. Most importantly, enduring trust is often only secured when the world turns ugly.

It was not until Herb had been retired for many years, that I finally understood the core reason we routinely put our trust in him. One afternoon I was listening to my First Officer forcefully discuss the current contract negotiations as we flew through the cloudless expanse of blue sky. If I recall correctly, we were in the third year of union and management hammering out a deal and, consequently, frustrations were running high. My First Officer was aggressively reminding me (the old guy in the cockpit) that we were no longer a smaller, low-cost carrier under Herb, but that we had morphed into a major domestic carrier, and as a result, it was time to fight hard to get what we deserved. I remember listening for a long time and then I looked him squarely in the eye and said, "My turn."

"You are correct," I said, turning to face him. "We were a low-cost and low-fare airline back then. And yes, our pilot wages were well below the top of the industry. And yes, there is no question Herb was a tough negotiator back then. And yes, back then, we pilots could have probably fought harder and gotten more money. But consider my career.

Over the last thirty years, I have never been *restructured*. I have never been through a bankruptcy. I have never been furloughed. I have never woken up in the middle of the night worrying about how I was going to pay my bills. You are correct that we certainly left money on the table with Herb, *but we trusted him to put those dollars back into the company. And he did just that.*

He kept our debt low and so we were well-positioned to succeed—in the good times, *and more importantly in the bad times, too.* Consequently, over the past thirty years, we never had to worry about job security. I am not trying to be boastful or tell you what to do, but my family feels that we've had a stable, wonderful ride. At times we fought bitterly with Herb, but I also have enjoyed coming to work most every day. What more can you ask of the big boss?"

My First Officer listened intently, thought for a while and asked, "Do you trust our current CEO?"

I smiled and said, "I'm nearing retirement. You have another twenty years here. That's a question only you can answer."

The act of having faith in your leader is knowing that in times of prosperity and success, he or she is preparing for the worst. Perhaps the most significant ingredient in transparent, responsible, and enduring leadership is being prepared for the worst. Specifically, this means that excess money and resources are routinely reinvested into the security and prosperity of the organization for the benefit of the employees, the customers, and the investors. Consequently, Herb never led SWA as a "get rich quick scheme." We were never harassed to "make our quarterly numbers," not even at times when sweeping global markets was the underlying business thesis in terms of maximizing shareholder value. I never heard Herb use those particular words, or anything close to them. He certainly did not think or act that way.

On the contrary, Herb was always playing the long game. He never leveraged our future by inflating revenues in the good times with excessive debt. He was supremely focused on our ability to power through the bad times. And we did, largely because we were always focused forward and prepared for the future. And what was the by-product of following a flight plan of financial responsibility versus a flight plan of financial engineering? It meant, for the most part, *we controlled our future.* In the good times, we, SWA under Herb, may have looked a little slow. But in the bad times, we were one of the strongest companies on the planet.

Prudent money management impacts everyone—families, communities, businesses, and societies. In a capitalistic society, the consequences of maximizing financial results in the short term with heavy debt loads tend to concentrate wealth toward the elite few at the top. In the long term, it's the larger group of working families that must pay the price.

In his later years at the helm, Herb boasted—always with a bellowing laugh and self-deprecating humor—that he had accurately predicted nine out of the last four recessions. The reality is Herb never knew when a recession (read: Big Risk) was coming. No one does. My airline and my family flew smoothly through two recessions with Herb, Colleen, and Jim at the helm. But each time, about a third of my friends and families at the other carriers were *restructured* through the bankruptcy courts.

Restructurings and Bankruptcies

Being restructured is a congenial enough sounding word. But in our industry, its actual meaning is that employees and their families get screwed. If the carrier survives, about one third of the employees are furloughed—which means laid off and/or fired. The employees who still have jobs lose about a third of their pay and benefits.

Here is how one of my First Officers recalls being restructured at another carrier: "We knew the airline was struggling. We were the one of the lowest paid in the industry and we had been in contract negotiations for four years. Our stock was falling. Rumors were rampant. On December 1, about 15% of the employees were furloughed, including me. Our oldest child was two years old and my wife was pregnant. Over the Christmas holidays, I heard from my friends who were still working that airline operations had melted down. Their airline was stranding thousands of people and families for days at airports across the country because the flying schedule had been aggressively increased, but there weren't enough pilots to fly the planes. The stock, however, rebounded nicely with increased revenues and lower costs. The CEO and CFO paid themselves multi-million-dollar bonuses for making the 'tough decisions' that helped turned around the airline. They screwed everyone and stole all the money. Merry Christmas."

Another pilot friend who was a senior pilot during the restructuring and furloughing his airline experienced, detailed the bankruptcy process at his airline. He managed to avoid being furloughed and never missed a paycheck, but his pay was significantly reduced, and his retirement package was also significantly reduced and altered.

What was his assessment? The bankruptcy was just another ruse for the same group of elite clowns to steal more money from working people. When the bankruptcy reached the court, who did the judge immediate authorize $500-an-hour payments to for another twelve to eighteen months? The exact same set of executives, lawyers, and consultants who had been crash-landing the airline for years. Not once did the judge ask any working employee what had happened or why.

Here's my take. In bankruptcy proceedings, most airline employees are represented by their unions, but unions are most often entrenched in trench warfare tactics, too. No one—including the union leaders—is interested in being cooperative or in understanding one another or problem-solving together. To working airline families, bankruptcy seems like just another high-stakes money grab, choreographed by the same group of protected, privileged, and wealthy winners. The rest of us all lose and pay the price, again and again. Perhaps this recurring feeling of frustration and hopelessness is one of the ingredients that caused the angry, worldwide populism movement to emerge.

When I discussed this topic with many of my nonairline friends, I quickly learned I was being naive and self-centered. Many privately held and publicly companies have experienced the same brutal restructuring, but the timing was significantly different. It was more like a lightning bolt, as previously valued employees were escorted off the premises by security teams with a cardboard box of personal items. An hour before, they had been called into meeting with HR, where they were informed that the company was going in a different direction and were then handed their severance package. During the brief meeting with HR, they were locked out of their computer and lost all company access.

Another friend, a mid-level executive with a highly successful twenty-five-year career at a large corporation, was forced by his boss, a senior vice president, to conduct two sets of terminations. He had to plan and write the script for the termination meetings according to exact specifications of corporate HR as well as the compliance attorney. He was actually forced to read the words he wrote to people he had worked with for years, many of whom were his close friends. The very act of doing so made him sick to his stomach. Six weeks after the second round of terminations, he was called into HR, where the HR person read him verbatim *the very same words he had written.* The same words he'd spoken to other members of his team. He knew the drill. He was off the property in fifteen minutes, and his boss of many years never even had to face him. Hopefully it is clear from these stories and the others that the worldwide, capitalistic practice of maximizing shareholder value has a singular focus, but far-reaching consequences.

So why did I veer off from talking about trust to maximizing shareholder value, restructurings, and financial engineering? From my perspective, these are powerful tools to increase profit margins and tip the scales of justice in favor of those who will benefit the most. These same systematic tools which are imbedded in our democratic society have produced structural wage and wealth inequality, resulting in those at the top becoming richer and more powerful.

But why do we continue to vote *for political leaders who support these same destructive practices that protect profit margins above our families?* In the long term, this weakens our society at its core. Most working families don't view our workplace environment as a level playing field, and as a result, many working families are losing hope in American capitalism. And the by-product of losing both trust and hope in mass amounts propels our society directly toward Big Risk.

Chapter Thirteen:

THE SECRET SAUCE

"You can make mistakes, but you aren't a failure until you start blaming others for those mistakes. When you blame others you are trying to excuse yourself. When you make excuses you can't evaluate yourself. Without proper self-evaluation, failure is inevitable."

—JOHN WOODEN, LEGENDARY COLLEGE
BASKETBALL COACH

In the previous chapter, I explained how important it is for employees to feel that the boss has their back, but what benefits or consequences does the organization, business, customers, or investors get from this sacred and trusting relationship? Well, it's hardly a secret. In fact, it's out there in plain sight for everyone to see. But yet, it is often overlooked, or discarded as immaterial.

I believe that the act of self-policing is the Secret Sauce. It acts as the linchpin between sustained success and continuous struggles—including sudden, Big Risk surprises. If that is not reason enough, self-policing also lowers costs and creates a smoother ride for everyone involved. After all, a group of individuals rarely self-polices itself without putting its implicit trust in the boss.

Many wise observers of personal character have observed that there are two fundamental ingredients of successful self-policing: self-reliance and self-discipline. If we are self-reliant and self-disciplined, we don't need to routinely rely on others for support. We can take care of ourselves and have the energy to support those around us—specifically our family and friends. Self-reliant and self-disciplined people can easily sidestep needless drama, and in general, most people gravitate toward those individuals who appear to be both self-reliant and self-disciplined in their daily lives.

The opposite of individuals who are self-reliant and self-disciplined are those who demonstrate needy behavior. Needy people often blame others and excessively vent about what happened to them. In contrast, self-discipline breeds integrity, confidence, and leadership and may be one of the most important human qualities that impacts the trajectory of a person's life. When individual team members are self-reliant and exercise self-discipline, a strong team is likely to emerge. When a group self-polices, that group is most likely to reach its highest states of productivity and reliability. When a group self-polices, it has the same impact on the group as it does on a single person regularly exercising self-discipline, but on a much larger scale. To take it a step further, when two of three people in a group have these qualities, the team now is equipped with a powerful engine.

When two out of three citizens of a democratic society have these qualities, that society controls its future. But like self-discipline, self-policing in a group is not easy to do or sustain. Speeches, branding visions, and measuring everything normally have little impact on the Secret Sauce. But actions do.

If a group cannot self-police, it often requires a much larger apparatus of human supervision to get employees to comply with written oversight documents. Without the Secret Sauce, the headcount, bureaucracy, and departments at headquarters must grow to monitor employee compliance. Without trust, the boss may feel the need to use authoritative law and order methods to get workers to follow orders. All these measures are costly, and often prove unreliable, and on top of this, every worker I have ever known has generally resented this type of work environment.

Basically, self-policing means *that the group knows what needs to be done and wants to make it happen.* When events go awry—and they always do—the nearest member of the group immediately handles the issue and the team keeps moving forward.

Herb Kelleher may have been the laziest CEO in the world. We employees did all the work and we did it gladly. *The employees were the powerful engine that powered SWA to great heights*—not that wacky, whiskey-drinking, rascal at top. Herb never empowered us, he just stayed the hell out of our way! He certainly never told pilots how to fly our airplanes. He certainly never told the mechanics how to fix our airplanes. And he certainly never hired supervisors with clipboards to hover over us. He had razor-thin supervisory ranks, and they stood next to us doing the same work, side by side.

Airlines face many problems every day, even on good days. When a problem did arise at SWA, the person nearest to it would address it immediately. If a problem was confusing or complex, two or three employees might huddle and discuss it for a minute or two. But an action plan was formulated quickly and soon it was back to work. Grit was a part of our DNA.

Most SWA employees could spot trouble from a mile away and proactively sidestep it. The important takeaway here is that *problems were not allowed to fester at SWA; they were immediately addressed head-on.* Most SWA employees had great Situational Awareness, people skills, and problem-solving skills, and those skills simply emerged from our trusting relationship with Herb, Colleen, and Jim.

Self-policing is about making timely course corrections without a lot of fuss or oversight. Each new Southwest employee learned to make timely course corrections from the example set by those around us and from those who came before us. Next to Herb, Colleen, and Jim, the majority of the credit for my successful career goes to the hard work and actions of pilots and employees who came before me. We were trained to proactively do our jobs the right way.

When Herb Got It Wrong

No one's perfect—even those we consider to be the most trustworthy among us. When I first began working for SWA, I could immediately sense that it was nothing like the rigid, grumpy atmosphere that permeated the post-Viet Nam peacetime military environment I'd just left. When I arrived for work each day at Southwest, people smiled at me and said hello when I walked down the corridors of our terminal—even on those mornings where I reported for duty at 4:30

a.m. A few months after joining the team, I attended my first union meeting—which proved to be a whole different kind of weird. It was clear that Southwest was a fun, vibrant, focused work environment, but in those meetings, I often sensed trouble brewing.

From what I could deduce, the Federal Aviation Administration (FAA) and Herb's airline were in a snit due to the fact that, back then, about half of our turn times were scheduled at ten-minute intervals. This means from the time an aircraft was parked at the jetway, that there was only a lag of ten minutes in total to unload passengers, reload passengers, and push back from the gate. To facilitate this effort, when the last passenger boarded, the tug driver would push the aircraft away from the jetway. A few minutes later, after the engines were started and the passengers were seated, the pilot would taxi the airplane to the runway. Herb argued that this strategy complied with the FAA regulations, which stated that all passengers must be seated before taxing the airplane. However, the FAA strongly disagreed. A legal battle then ensued—or so thought Herb, who was also a highly accomplished lawyer.

The FAA reached deep into their tool box and began to charge Captains individually with Regulation 91.9, which states that a Captain cannot fly an airplane *in a reckless or dangerous manner.* The FAA can use this powerful regulation when *their gazillion other frigging regulations do not hold up in a court of law.* Unsurprisingly, it worked. The FAA won. SWA stopped pushing back with people standing. Herb lost ... but he was also in danger of losing the trust of his pilots.

Herb may have miscalculated, but he soon recovered. At my very first union meeting, Herb and the pilots had a "heated" chat, eye-to-eye, where everyone got an opportunity to have their say. Herb admitted when he was wrong and had miscalculated and agreed to pay all the union's lawyer fees. Most importantly, Herb learned from his mistake. For his remaining years as CEO, there were a few more heated family chats, but the trust between the pilots and the CEO was never threatened again.

Good Bosses Need Respect Too

I deeply believe SWA, under Herb, Colleen, and Jim, was a great American company. Perhaps, I am biased or was lucky to work for them, or maybe even both. In describing those days, I'm not trying to brag, but rather I'm attempting to deconstruct why things at Southwest seemed to work so well. The reality is, back then, I often felt like I was running with a band of misfits but having the best time of my life in doing so. Herb was a wacky, brilliant freak of nature, but he was a great boss. And even back then, I sensed that great bosses were very rare indeed.

Good bosses, however, are not rare, and they need to be respected and appreciated, too. From the outside, running a business doesn't look easy. It often resembles a kind of organized chaos, much like parenting with three kids: investors, employees, and customers. All three need to be nurtured and all three are continuously competing for attention. Since I have spent most of my working life studying large-group dynamics and listening to employees, I've learned along the way that most employee comments can be distilled to three fundamental questions:

1. How does the boss treat me?

2. How does the boss run the operations or provide the goods or service?

3. How well has the boss positioned the organization or corporation for the future?

Again, the scoring of the questions is key. Collectively, if the employees are answering any one of the questions positively, then the boss gets one point, and the tipping point is a score of two. From my observations, if a boss was a receiving a score of two, he or she was doing a good job, but most employees often did not see it that way and receiving a score of three was nearly impossible.

When I was writing my newsletter for the investment community, I was invited to many brokerage conferences for investors in New York City. After attending a three-day event in New York City and then immediately turning around to fly a four-day week as a Captain for SWA, my head was spinning. I told my wife that I was working in two completely different realities. Between attending the airline conference and actually flying a passenger airplane, I did not hear one comment, concern, topic, or data point that overlapped between my two worlds. Nothing I heard or saw while flying was of any interest to investors, and nothing I heard from investors seemed to be of any interest to employees or passengers.

One evening I was flying back on American Airlines to Dallas–Fort Worth from an investor conference in Manhattan, and riding in the extra seat in the cockpit, commonly referred to as the jump seat. After reaching our cruising altitude, the three of us started chatting, and I mentioned to the Captain that I'd been at a conference in New York where their CEO had spoken. At this time, the pilots and the CEO at that particular airline were embroiled in heated negotiations.

As I spoke, I noticed that the tension in the cockpit rose a bit as the Captain tried to figure out if I stood with labor or with management.

The Captain wanted to know if I had reported in my newsletter how difficult their CEO had been to the pilots. I said, yes. I had specifically reported the internal skirmishes and the union's concerns about pay and benefits to investors. The tension then subsided and we were best friends again. I agreed that they worked for a tough boss.

Unfortunately the employees, collectively, did not grade the same way I did. At the time, Bob Crandall was the CEO of American Airlines. Clearly, Crandall only got two votes from the pilots on this analysis scale. They used to say, "Bob Crandall is an asshole, but he's *our* asshole." Bob and the pilots fought bitterly, but the pilots believed that Bob ran a good airline and positioned American Airlines well for its future endeavors. Looking back now, Crandall successful accomplished both tasks and may have been one of our industry's most successful CEOs. He pioneered many insights that are still integral parts of our industry today. At that time, Bob Crandall earned the respect of the pilots *and* his two votes, but that doesn't mean he was necessarily appreciated while he was in charge.

When Crandall left, the pilots smiled, if not cheered, even though the next CEO was completely ineffective. After that, American Airlines chose a CEO who genuinely tried to run a good airline profitably, while also taking good care of employees. But at best, he only scored a one-and-a-half—getting a half point on all three questions. During his extended CEO tenure, American Airlines lost its edge and focus. The 2008 financial meltdown hurt the airline, and in 2011, American Airlines, and all its employees, landed in bankruptcy.

In hindsight, I wonder if the American Airlines employees would have preferred to have Bob Crandall at the helm for a longer period of time, if they'd had the chance to do so. This is another instance when this timeless lesson applies: "Be careful what you wish for. You just might get it."

Perhaps I seem harsh in my judgment of American Airlines and its employees. Perhaps I am. Perhaps I am not. I live next to DFW, and many of my closest personal friends are American Airlines employees. Watching their struggles back then, and now with COVID-19, is nothing to cheer about. It is gut-wrenching to watch good, hardworking families suffer continuously.

Perhaps my memory is jaded. It probably took me longer to learn and appreciate the Kelleher Trust Doctrine and the Secret Sauce than I originally conveyed. At Southwest, we were in a unique position in that we believed in Herb, Colleen, and Jim, and they believed in us. We flew well together. I naively thought that if all members of the team simply worked hard and trusted one another, this paradigm could be easy replicated. In retrospect, I probably held onto this vision a bit too tightly as well.

PART FOUR: ARE WE TRAVELING IN THEWRONG DIRECTION?

Chapter Fourteen:

A PILOT'S LIST OF BIG RISK

"Resentment is like drinking poison and expecting your enemies to die."

—Nelson Mandela

Over twenty years ago, my wife was diagnosed with breast cancer. After the surgery, we met with the oncologist, who explained that her job was to kill any fast-growing cancer cells that might be left behind. She then took her thumb and index fingers, holding them a half an inch apart, looked at me, and said, "To ensure we get every last mutating cancer cell, I'm going to come *this* close to killing your wife." Thankfully, that is exactly what she did, and my wife not only survived but has been cancer-free ever since.

I believe the biggest risk to our future is that we face it as a divided society, infected with Trench Warfare Dementia, which means that our minds are closed, and we are continually hoarding resources from one another. The consequences of such a reality can be severe. As a result, we are poorly prepared to perform well in the future. Hell, America is not even focused forward as a general rule!

In Part Four of this book, I will attempt to cut out the cancer of Trench Warfare Dementia and administer a round of social chemotherapy to rid ourselves of any remaining fast-growing cancerous cells, so we can return to a healthy society. *We also need to rebuild our Good Guys Team*, which I believe is the best flight plan we can utilize to take care of ourselves, our families, our communities, and our country. *I am 100% confident that we possess the problem-solving skills in order to work together to meet the Big Risk looming in our future*, but first we must pull our head out of our collective asses without delay. The reality is that as human beings living on earth, *we are more interconnected than ever*. Whether we like it or not, *we are all in this together*, and it is time we started acting like it.

In this book, I have detailed my observations, experiences, and training throughout my years as a pilot and a human being, but I have purposely refrained from giving my personal opinions on specific issues or from trying to sway readers toward my worldview. I still have no desire, *and no need to change anyone personal opinions or sway their worldview*. But make no mistake about it—I do plan to use the biggest crowbar and sledgehammer I can find to dislodge us from the miserable squalor of strident trenches, and shove all of us Good Guys back into the prosperous, wide-open space of the middle ground.

The strongest chemotherapy I will utilize is the concept of self-policing.

Big Risk

When I first started writing this book, after explaining the concept to my son, he looked at me and said, with no small amount of exasperation, "Dad, all I hear you talk about are *problems*. I want to hear about solutions we can actually *use*."

I pondered his words for almost two years before arriving at a path toward those solutions. (Dear Son, I realize that at this point I am still talking about problems, not solutions. The first step—and most vital step—to solving a problem is recognizing we indeed have a problem! The second step is to first get some kind of grasp on reality. Please keep reading to the end. I promise I will eventually offer solutions—kinda.)

But back to the issue at hand. How can a Captain and a First Officer work well together in the cockpit on every single flight to ensure safe landings when they know that one of them voted for Hillary and the other for Trump? The answer is powerfully simple. In the back of both of their minds, they know that if they fail to work together effectively in this present moment, the consequences will be enormous. Simply put? They could die. Petty political and social issues become meaningless when you know you only have one chance to get things right.

One of the impacts of becoming infected with Trench Warfare Dementia is that the entire energy and focus in our society is on fighting one another. No one's radar is focused outward anymore. As a result, Big Risk can waltz right in undetected, and no one will see it coming. Consequently, the most important lesson of the Big Risk Doctrine—*turn away before getting too close*—never happens. No one even discusses it.

Three Tribes

To navigate this flight path or "thought experiment" of injecting high doses of social chemotherapy directly into both trenches, hopefully *without pissing everyone off,* I am going to lead this discussion by creating three tribes. Each reader can *choose* the characteristics of whichever tribe they most identify with. To add clarity, without adding confrontation or being judgmental, I will use the observations of my own family, friends, and life to create these tribes. Any resemblance to my kinfolk is purely coincidental.

My wife and I are truly blessed. We both have had successful, loving, and supportive parents. My father was a military officer and my parents voted as conservative Republicans most of their lives. My wife's parents (they are both deceased) were highly educated, successful small business owners and were more liberal thinking and often voted democratic. After almost forty years of being married to my loving wife, these "roots" of our marriage still run deep.

My tribe is often made up pilots, ex-military, Texans, church-going Christians, and gun owners. All these characteristics are naturally who I am, and for most of my life, I have voted as a fiscally responsible, conservative Republican.

My wife's tribe is also fiscally responsible but is more liberal on social issues. She believes the National Rifle Association (NRA) is irresponsibly evil. She respects others' faiths, but believes that organized religion has often been used by men to repress women. Around twenty years ago, my wife detected the ugly, authoritative wind swirling around conservative, Christian Texas Republicans, and ever since that moment, she has voted exclusively Democratic. As she puts it, however, in North Texas, the home of Tea Party, her vote has never counted. Under the Electoral College apparatus and because of abusive, gerrymandering judges claiming to follow the constitution and conservative politicians protecting a "good-old-boy network," my wife's assertion is correct. For the past twenty years in North Texas, her vote *has* never really counted.

The third tribe is fictitious but patterned after biblical history—the lost tribes of Israel. I have included three notions that were once a set of fundamental values or beliefs or skills that propelled the American society forward, societal attributes which have long been eradicated from our minds as a result of infectious Trench Warfare Dementia:

1. Citizenship
2. The U.S. taxpayer
3. Yankee ingenuity

My Big Risk List

Here comes my personal list of the Big Risk facing our society today. Note that this is my own personal list and I doubt any reader would create one that is exactly the same, but moving forward, we will use this list as placeholder for *really bad stuff* we would never want to impact our families.

1. Debt and denial
2. Too much hatred and too many bullets

3. Our theological, ideological, and economic denial of science—thus negating responsible medical practices and our responsibility to care for the planet

4. Concentration of wealth—the corruption of capitalist economic systems

5. Concentration of power—the corruption of democratic political systems

As I see it, the number one threat to America's future is *debt and denial.* My tribe used to be extremely concerned with the mountain of U.S. debt, which seems to grow larger every day, but the current reality is that those days are long gone. Citizens, democracies, and capitalists also used to worry about excessive borrowing. But these days, to keep *our consumer-powered* and *maximizing shareholder value investor-driven* economy humming along, our federal government, corporations, and banks now *feel entitled* to unlimited borrowing at an interest rate of zero.

Our constitution states that it is the responsibility of Congress to properly finance the goods and services which the government provides to its citizens, but now, this task has been outsourced to the Federal Reserve. To keep the mirage of our strong economy intact, the wealthiest investors, donors, and corporations have intimidated the Federal Reserve into using just two money spigots—open and *wide open*, which only leads to more debt.

Unknowingly, we have backed ourselves—and the foundation of our capitalistic economy—into a dangerous corner.

The Federal Reserve's original charter was put in place solely to manage the supply of cash for economic stability. Under these original guidelines, they had several powerful tools to work with. The Federal Reserve could lower interest rates to stimulate the economy and increase growth. They could also raise interests to cool down the economy and fight inflation. With our increased debt load, however, the Federal Reserve cannot appreciably raise rates, because there is no way the American Government or American taxpayer would be able to meet the financial burden of increased interest payments.

Over the past twenty years, the Federal Reserve, or Fed, has had to redefine the official "inflation rate" several times. Each time the Fed has redefined the official inflation rate, which measures the cost of a standard list of goods and services items theoretically purchased each month by a typical American family, the inflation rate has magically been lowered. Now the official inflation rate is retitled as "core inflation." The reason for this new and improved inflation rate is simple math. Each time the official inflation rate has been redefined— seemly with the full support from both parties in Washington—it is because the Fed simple drop items from the list they counted. They justified their truncated list of monthly family purchases because the dropped items were creating too much volatility or "noise" for their macroeconomic models. Now, core inflation in the United States does not include food or energy costs—that volatility, liability and responsibility has been exclusively outsourced to American families, but not our government.

Also over the last generation, our corporate leaders have outsourced the *investment liability* of retirement back to American families when they bankrupted pensions and shifted to 401Ks. This hidden agenda magically pushed the retirement funds of American families directly back into the hands of banks. Now when investing in the stock market, the banks are to first extract their reliable income stream, while conveniently leaving the more volatile investment liability to mom and dad.

This is why I consider our burgeoning debt the number one threat to the American society. This Big Risk has significant global concerns, too. Since the Bretton Woods Agreement after the end of World War II, the value of the U.S. dollar has been the stabilizing foundation of the global economy. To keep this Ponzi scheme humming along, our federal government could start printing more money, but history is clear. America would eventually default, and as a result, the global economy would collapse, thus triggering worldwide anarchy.

Please remember, at the very start of this book, I warned against flying directly toward Big Risk, as it can overwhelm us, creating a situation that is not about stability, but survival.

It should be obvious to anyone paying attention that the wealth and power of our elite investors, donors, and corporations—principally via my tribe and its lobbyists—have also put the U.S. Congress in lockdown. These elite power brokers' primary tool to lower their expenses is to surreptitiously carve up the U.S. tax code to their liking, which only leads to more debt.

To counterbalance the ways in which my tribe has pampered and protected the wealthiest of us in our society for the past twenty years, many in my wife's tribe are now naturally calling for American families to be given single-payer healthcare and free college education. Which will lead us to ... yup, more debt.

The reality is that we Americans now feel we are entitled to borrow funds on an unlimited basis. When the COVID-19 bailout was created for businesses across America, I heard dozens of bankers and pundits refer to it as "free money." "You'd be foolish not to take it," they said. These bailouts were certainly needed, but that "free money" was just more debt. Making matters worse, our Treasury refused to properly account for this distribution. Our government—directly driven by the White House—passed out a half of trillion dollars of U.S. debt and said it was "proprietary information," so our highest governmental leaders did not need to tell us—the working families—who they gave the money to! Which is just unbelievable! These types of divine rights are normally only afforded to fascist dictators.

The reality is that America—all of us, really—seem addicted to both debt *and denial.* We realize that increasing debt loads can hurt our families and businesses. So why are we still in denial that it can't harm our country?

The whole reason I wrote the Big Risk Doctrine in Part One was to get us—the Good Guys—to recognize the fact that we are getting too close to an economic collapse, and as a result, we need to make a major course correction, NOW!

Later, I will make some suggestions on what those corrections might look like.

More Evidence—In Plain Sight

For now, I would like to offer more evidence to support my notion that we are flying too close to Big Risk, and as a result, it's now time to turn away. But before we go any further, I would *please* like every reader to put down this book and visit the website www.usdebtclock. org. Look closely at the rapidly exploding numbers, which are promises we—the American people and the American taxpayer—have made to a person, family, or entity.

Look at *all that unfunded debt! Trillions of dollars of it!* That should scare the crap out of anyone—in *any* tribe or trench. Hell, if the U.S. dollar is holding up the global economy, then everyone on the planet should be nervous—not just U.S. taxpayers. For this pilot, the spinning numbers on the U.S. Debt Clock website represent our future. As I've mentioned earlier in this book, using denial while flying an airplane is a fatal flaw. I am deeply concerned that the mixture of debt and denial will be the fatal flaw of my generation.

I listed my five Big Risks above, but thus far I have only supported the first risk: debt and denial. However, I firmly believe that all five Big Risks are intertwined, and the current flight path that our divided society is traveling upon appears to be producing several dangerous consequences as a result.

Searching for Reality—More Reading Material

I have spent a lifetime researching this book, but most of my supporting data points come from experiences and observations, while my understanding has heavily leaned on the wisdom of others. Today we, as a society, seem to get most of our "news" or data points to make decisions instantly presented on TV and social media; which is deeply bifurcated and prepackaged. I believe America—to our detriment—is overlooking a valuable source of thought-provoking, well researched knowledge from non-fiction books and other illuminating open-minded material. America used to be a nation of readers and thinkers. Now we seem to do a lot of watching, clicking and posting.

The following is a list of the gifted authors and thinkers. I appreciate their efforts to critically search for reality, which greatly enhances our situational awareness.

John Mauldin is an economist, devout capitalist, author, and investment advisor who writes a free weekly newsletter that anyone can sign up for at his website, www.mauldineconomics.com. Mauldin's intellectual strength is that he does not deny debt, but consistently addresses it. This is probably the number one reason why he isn't more popular with the general public. He seeks to understand not only our current reality but also where we may be headed as a result.

Jonathan Tepper, another devout capitalist, recently published a book entitled *The Myth of Capitalism*. Tepper writes extensively about the revolving door between corporate leaders and government industry regulatory positions. As Tepper explains it, the corporations handsomely reward a person who can seamlessly transition from industry to federal industry regulator and back to industry. His book is an insightful read and pulls back the curtain on *crony capitalism*.

In my opinion, one of the finest books ever written about wealth and its tendency to covertly pull powerful economic strings in our society is Jane Mayer's *Dark Money: The Hidden History of the Billionaires Behind the Rise of the Radical Right*, which details the huge sums of cash which currently manipulate public opinion: "The network has brought together some of the richest people on the planet. Their core beliefs—that taxes are a form of tyranny; that government oversight of business is an assault on freedom—are sincerely held. But these beliefs also advance their personal and corporate interests: Many of their companies have run afoul of federal pollution, worker safety, securities, and tax laws."

Mayer's book was published in 2016, but it wouldn't surprise me if this same wealthy, elitist network Mayer refers to has also cleverly concocted today's catchy phrases such as "fake news," "deep state," and "it's a hoax." These endlessly repeated claims from the dark corners of conservative media are designed to viciously assault any democratic or regulatory institution they deem annoying or irrelevant or that is costing them money.

In 2018, Adam Winkler wrote a brilliant historical examination of how American corporations, from the very beginning of our existence, have used our judicial courts to gain an overwhelming advantage over American families by manipulating the U.S. Constitution. His book, *We the Corporation—How American Business Won Their Civil Rights*, explores the idea that our founding fathers *never* intended corporations to have any civil rights. As Winkler puts it, civil rights are for people, not business entities. According to Winkler, in 1776, our revered founding fathers created our great nation and wrote our landmark U.S. Constitution, but these accomplishments did embrace two bitter compromises. They punted on slavery and women's right to vote—actions that are still impacting our society today.

In an illuminating story Winkler writes that in 1868 after the Civil War, the 14th amendment of our constitution was passed, giving citizenship to former slaves and guaranteeing all citizens "equal protection of the laws." Congressman and prized lawyer, Roscoe Conkling, was a member of the Congressional committee that actually penned the 14th amendment. Many years later, after all the other members of the committee who wrote the 14th amendment had died, Conkling successfully argued to the Supreme Court that the 14th amendment actually intended to include the idea of extending equal protection of the *law to corporations!* His arguments were later proved to be outright lies, but his efforts that day—for which he was richly paid—gave corporations more civil rights which they still hold today.

Perhaps the most brilliantly researched book about the hidden powerful forces masterfully manipulating our politics, courts and society today is *Democracy in Chains—The Deep History of the Radical Right's Stealth Plan for America*, written by Nancy MacLean. Maclean writes: "in a last-gasp attempt to preserve the power of white elite in the wake of Brown v. Board of Education…right-wing corporate donors and their foundations were only too eager to support… teaching others how to divide the citizenry into 'makers' and 'takers'. On a messianic mission to rewrite the social contract of the modern world, multibillionaires…deployed a vast, many-armed apparatus [and a Nobel Prize economist] to carry to out their strategy."

My two favorite books about 2008 economic meltdown are *All the Devils Are Here—The Hidden History of the Financial Crisis* by Bethany McLean and Joe Nocera and *The End of Alchemy—Money, Banking and the Future of the Global Economy* by Mervyn King.

McLean and Nocera's *All the Devils Are Here* goes behind the scenes of the clueless, American, Wall Street investment community. At this time, the banks all had modeling tools which stated that they held a manageable amount of liability. These same banks had created rapid-fire, complex financial instruments and were making a fortune frantically trading them in unregulated, derivative markets. At the time of the meltdown, our economy (GDP) was about fifteen trillion dollars. McLean and Nocera heard about estimates of the size of these unregulated derivative markets of hundreds of trillion dollars. The reality was no one—bankers, regulators, or investors—understood what was going on. While the music was blaring, everyone was happy and getting rich. Then the credit markets froze, revealing yet another house of cards, which the Federal Reserve and the American taxpayer had to bailout.

Mervyn King acted as the head of the Bank of England for ten years, before, during, and after the 2008 financial meltdown. His book, *The End of Alchemy—Money, Banking, and the Future of the Global Economy*, explains these complex financial arrangements so simply that even a pilot can understand them. King writes, "When giving evidence to the Treasury Select Committee in the House of Commons, I would sometimes respond to questions by saying, 'I don't know, I don't have a crystal ball.'

Such an answer outraged many Members of Parliament. They thought it was my job to have an official crystal ball in order to tell them what the future held. Any attempt to explain that not only could I not forecast the future, but neither could they, and for that matter could anyone else, was regarded with disbelief. Down the ages, quack doctors selling patent medicines and astrologer selling predictions have been in strong demand. Added to their number today are economists selling forecasts, reflecting a desire for certainty that is as irrational as it is understandable."

King's book is one of the finest economic works I have ever read, but make no mistake, the reason I respect King is because of his truthful candor regarding financial issues. As King points out, I am not sure whether we humans demand to be told with certainty what the future holds, or whether we are easily fooled by someone claiming they can predict that future.

For all of us, life will be filled with Big Risk. The God of our faith, our governments, and institutions must be alert for Big Risk and assist us with dealing with it. Still the reality remains, *it is the job and responsibility of the people of the society to recognize Big Risk when it is in plain sight and demand we turn away from it.*

Chapter Fifteen:

SOMETHING IS WRONG

"You can imprison a man, but not an idea. You can exile a man, but not an idea. You can kill a man, but not an idea."

—BENAZIR BHUTTO

At first glance, this selection of observations and comments may seem unrelated, but they are in fact necessary in helping illuminate the fundamental reasons that the American society is experiencing such difficulty moving forward.

My father-in-law, David Miller, was a Harvard Business School graduate and one of the most intelligent, hardworking men I have known. In 1964, with Mr. Smith, he started and ran a successful home-building business in the Washington D.C. area for many years. That business, Miller and Smith, is still building quality homes more than fifty-five years later.

In the early 1990s, Dave started another homebuilding business with his son, his daughter (my wife), and me—just before a nasty recession. After four tough years we made it work, but it was not easy or fun. Recessions are a fact of life in the home-building industry, and without Dave and his wife Pat's support—and their financial wherewithal—we would have failed.

During these tough times, our federal income tax returns included plenty of losses and quickly became complicated. On several occasions, I turned to Dave for tax guidance. Finally, in what I sensed was his deep frustration, he told me that he had no idea what our tax consequences were! Yes, he had read the current tax code laws many times over trying to calculate their consequences, but each year the same scenario unfolded. He ended up simply turning over all his business records to an accountant and held his breath.

Something is very wrong when a man of Dave's intelligence, character, and skills cannot understand our income tax code, no matter how many times he reads it.

Fishing Buddies

A few years ago I attended a surprise 60th birthday celebration for a good friend. The room was teeming with partygoers—there must've been a hundred people in the room. Everyone shared funny stories of my friend's life, and as I listened, I couldn't help admiring the path he had chosen in life. He and his wife were hardworking, churchgoing people who had raise four great kids in our neighborhood. When my wife was diagnosed with breast cancer years earlier, it was my friend's wife who'd organized the meal train that brought a stream of nourishing meals to our home. These folks walked humbly. At the surprise party, I overhead a guest say, "There's not a bad bone in his body. He's one of the finest men I know."

For several years, he and I embarked on an annual fly-fishing trip together. One cold, early morning, the two of us were driving to his favorite fishing hole in Montana. We were casually discussing a recent terrorist attack orchestrated by a Muslim extremist group. Without missing a beat, my friend looked over at me calmly and said, "It's not surprising I guess, considering that Muslims hate us and want to kill us."

I was stunned.

After a moment of silence, I composed myself and quietly said, "Do you really believe that *all* Muslims hate us and want to kill us?"

He answered, not in an angry voice, but in a matter of fact tone, one that told me he was quite sure of the validity of his answer, "Maybe not all of them, but I am assuming most of them do."

I then promptly changed the subject to tying flies. In hindsight, I wish I would have asked where he formed this belief. Was it from his church, news media, or friends? But the bottom line is that when one of the humblest, good-natured Christians I know systematically believes another billion people who worship the same God and share the same father (Abraham) want to kill us, *then something is very wrong.*

This is not the only time I have heard a similar sentiment from many of my Christian friends. Now, when I hear these apocryphal, apocalyptic comments, I usually mumble something like, "Yeah … it sounds like the Christian Crusades all over again."

Teaching My Kids to Save

This is another well-intentioned effort in parenting that badly missed the mark. It happens … a lot. When my two kids reached adolescence, my wife and I took them to our local bank and opened up individual savings accounts in their name. I put five hundred dollars in each account, with visions of that money growing to five thousand dollars over the next fifty years. When we got home, we had several family discussions about the power of saving a little money each month to add to the fund, and it growing over time. The plan was for each kid to then routinely contribute a small amount to their respective accounts.

That was the plan. However, we executed it rather poorly. In fact, everyone—including myself—completely forgot about the savings account! Later, after both of our kids graduated from college, left our home, got good jobs, and married wonderful spouses, and many years after we setup the original accounts and the bank had changed its name three or four times, my son sent me the bank statement for his savings account. We had never made any additional contributions or requested any investment advice, but the bank(s) were paying interest the entire time on the original sum. The total interest, after ten-plus years of compounding interest payments, *was fifty-eight cents.* I write this story not to highlight poor parenting techniques—but *to highlight deceptive banking practices.*

During about this same period, we experienced a financial meltdown. In 2008 nearly every major American bank froze or failed due to deceptive banking practices in unregulated markets, but *not one banker went to jail.* Not one! As a hardworking American family that needs to save and invest for our health, well-being, and retirement, this makes me angry.

Also since then the Federal Reserve has been forced to let banks borrow money at near-zero interest rates the entire time.

Before the coronavirus, because of the fragile economic environment, many economists expected to see near-zero interest rates for many years. Now with the loss of life, loss of jobs, and economic destruction from the virus, we may see near-zero interest rates continue on for *decades*.

One of the consequences, or by-products, of this continued structural bailout of banks is that American families receive what amounts to zero interest on their bank savings accounts—just like my kids. Since the Great Depression, one of the primary ways American families prepared for retirement was using saving accounts with compounding interest that steadily grew over time. Now, the kinds of savings techniques we used in the past to grow our wealth have been hijacked by those seeking higher returns from the stock market in 401k accounts. And who controls the trading in the stock market, thus receiving huge upfront transaction fees? Yup, you guessed it: the banks. This structural change in our economy—which seems to directly parallel the economic stagnation of the American family— was quietly shepherded in during the late 1990s by lobbyists convincing (controlling) Congress.

During one of my many mediocre, entrepreneurial attempts, I was working as a Registered Investment Advisory at a small local asset management firm. While studying for the securities exam, however, I was stunned to find out that much of our current securities laws were originally instituted directly after the Great Depression, a period when most banks had failed. This legislation, also known as the Glass–Steagall Act, completely separated the banking industry into three clearly defined, and strictly regulated, industries: banks for general public savings, investment banks, and insurance.

The banks for general public savings were federally regulated and federally backed by the FDIC or Federal Deposit Insurance Corporation. The investment banks were lightly regulated, but not insured. Clients of investment banks were limited to wealthier clients willing *to take more risk in unregulated markets.* The insurance industry was created, which was highly regulated and only allowed customers to invest in regulated securities with minimal risk. The bottom line is that at this time in American history, savings, investing, and insurance were completely separated.

The Glass–Steagall laws worked well in America for almost seventy years with no major financial disruptions in banks, investing, or insurance. However, in 1999, with an overwhelming assault by powerful banking lobbyists on Congress, the Glass–Steagall Act was repealed, and less than ten years later, we endured the economic meltdown of 2008, when our banks again failed or froze. Why? It's simple. All of our banks collectively held trillions of complex savings, investing, and insurance schemes in unregulated markets that no one understood, or even knew who ultimately held the liability.

Something is very wrong.

Labeling Others

I was talking to a frustrated millennial a few months ago, a member of my wife's tribe who clearly despised our current administration. "Anyone that supports the White House is either stupid, lazy, mean or won't do their own research!" He said while throwing up his hands in an expression of complete exasperation.

I found his statement odd. Why exactly? Because I knew for a fact that both of his parents supported the current White House administration in question! Not only did they support the administration and our current President, but they were also highly educated, intelligent, hardworking people, and good friends to all who had the pleasure of knowing them.

One of the most frequent comments I often hear—from both sides—is *those people are too lazy to do their own research*. I guess one of the attributes of a society infected with Trench Warfare Dementia is that only people who agree with us do their own research! And to that point, all those who happen to disagree with us are just too lazy or stupid to research much of anything in general.

Something seems very wrong when each tribe or trench routinely labels the other as lazy and stupid. Maybe we have forfeited our keen Situational Awareness skills and allowed the barking trench commanders to place their altered reality into our heads. Maybe, as a society, we have outsourced critical thinking to loudest, most strident, and hateful voices.

Tying Ourselves in Knots

I have never flown a combat mission, but I did technically participate in the Cold War. Like my father before me, I was in the Strategic Air Command (SAC), which back then was the branch of the Air Force that controlled both the nuclear missile launchers and nuclear B-52 bombers. Being in SAC meant we sat "alert." This meant every third week, the flight crews lived—twenty-four hours a day, seven days a week—in a building located a hundred yards from the planes. We were prepared to get airborne, within a few minutes of being notified, to fly our strategic missions.

SAC's stated mission was deterrence, and it worked. Thankfully, no one launched any nukes, as the retaliatory capabilities of each side were at too high a cost. The Cold War started when the Iron Curtain fell in 1991. In the 1980s, President Reagan increased military spending, which the USSR tried to match. Our economy could handle the increased debt load, but the Russian economy could not. The Russian economy collapsed, the wall fell, and the Cold War was over.

I am wondering if a second Cold War has now begun, but this time, perhaps we are fighting with electronic data instead of nuclear bombs. According to all the U.S. intelligence communities, our 2016 Presidential Election was interfered with by Russian software engineers (hackers) placing millions of false posts on Facebook. Naturally, since our society is infected with Trench Warfare Dementia, neither trench nor tribe agrees on what actually occurred. We cannot agree on facts or the truth. Since my tribe won the election, many in my tribe deny this attack occurred or it had any meaningful impact. Our President did ask Russian President Vladimir Putin three times publicly, but Voldemort … I mean, Vladimir, agreed with our current President that it did not happen.

Not surprisingly, my wife's tribe, the side that lost, disagrees with the guy who won *and* the Russian President. Instead, her tribe agrees with the U.S. intelligence community and every reputable news organization.

In many American minds and in dark corners of alt-right barking trench commanders, this battle still rages on. If a second Cold War has broken out, Vladimir Putin has struck first by using strategic military weaponry—false Facebook posts. Without firing a single shot or costing his country one piece of expensive military equipment, he effectively tied the American public in knots where we still remain, hunkered down and fighting one another from our separate trenches. Magically, Voldemort has ultimately made the American public forget just how the first Cold War was lost—with a crushing amount of debt.

History repeats itself. So does Big Risk.

Fascism

In 2018, Madeleine Albright wrote *Fascism—A Warning*, a topic she understood intimately through her own firsthand experience. At a young age, Albright's family was chased out of her native Czechoslovakia, not once, but twice: once by Hitler and again by the communists. In her role as U.S. Secretary of State from 1997 to 2001, she began to sense that once again, the seeds of fascism were being planted around the world. In her book, Albright describes a fascist leader as, "someone who claims to speak for a whole nation or group, is utterly unconcerned with the rights of others, and is willing to use violence and whatever other means are necessary to achieve the goals he or she might have." Former Secretary Albright is now clearly, deeply concerned about America, and with extremely good reason.

Growing up, my wife, Beth—she's the smart one of the family—read and enjoyed many dystopian novels. Now, whenever she hears Republican leaders dodge questions with quips about "fake news" or "the deep state," or "it's a hoax," she'll exclaim, "That's how they did it in all the dystopian novels! They destroy all the democratic institutions to gain absolute control of the media and military." It seems that throughout history, many despotic leaders have risen

to power by gaining control of three power[...]
tary, and the church. The very same instituti[...]
designed to protect and promote hardworkin[...]
used to pound us into submission.

I was reminded of these same levers las[...]
Trump, with the Attorney General and a mi[...] at his side, ordered the U.S. military to forcefully disperse a peaceful crowd so he could get a photo-op with *a Bible* in front of an empty church.

Are Our Markets Addicted to Sugar Pills?

Our stock markets may not be completely rigged against a family attempting to save for its future, but it is abundantly clear that investors demand a sugar pill from publicly traded corporations during earnings season, which comes every quarter and lasts for six weeks. Today's markets aren't driven by creating sustainable value but are powered by short-term consumerism and an edict that maximizes shareholder value. To reinforce this addiction, Wall Street investors demand that corporate CEOs "make their numbers" every quarter. Wall Street investors will also reward or punish CEOs if macroeconomic news *momentarily* favors or does not favor their corporate vision.

I started my career working for a small corporation, and now thirty years later, I work for a large corporation with millions of customers, and more than fifty thousand employees, at a company that generates huge streams of revenue. Any notion that every three months our CEO can make a significant change or create a new income stream is preposterous! It's also preposterous that he has

influence over the activity of our competitors, the price
t fuel), or the general economy.

From my perspective of working inside such a corporation, it
probably takes between twelve and eighteen months for even the most
nimble of large corporations to effectively make a significant course
correction. In reality, when the CEO does makes an announcement
on an earnings call that the market favors, out comes the army of
headquarters folks gathering data to document its success in order
to properly impress its investors.

Essentially four times a year, our market demands that CEOs
carefully skirt the laws, creatively lie, and deliver investors a sugar
pill—also known as a placebo. CEOs who can't consistently "make
their numbers" are often sacked after only a few years. But no worries. They always land safely via a lavish, golden parachute.

The Consequences of Making Your Numbers

The pressure "to make your numbers" can produce dangerous consequences, but before we get into those, first I'd like to offer a lesson
about why airplanes are so incredible safe. There are many reasons
the aviation industry has such enviable safety record, but for this
story I will focus on the brilliant work of qualified aeronautical engineers who design and build airplanes. Like pilots, they often learned
their craft the hard way. What's their Secret Sauce? They design *triple redundancy systems* for all aircraft primary systems, and then
wire and power them independently. This is the fundamental reason
every airplane (mostly Boeings) my father and I have flown have
always brought us home safely. In my mind, there is no greater fundamental reason for airplane design reliability and safety than triple

redundancy. This is why I have always been thankful that I exclusively fly Boeings.

Until now…

Recently, the two crashes of the Boeing 737 Max abruptly exposed what I believe should be considered criminal neglect. (Just for full disclosure, my airline was a launch customer for the Boeing 737 Max and I personally flew the Max, as a Captain, several times before it was grounded.) The Boeing 737 Max was designed with a pitch override system with a single-point sensor. To make matters worse, this system was designed to fail from the very start due to one simple fact: they *never implemented triple redundancy into such a powerful override system.* The pitch override was purposely designed to be the lowest-cost solution, one that disregarded every reliability and safety tenet every aeronautical engineer is taught on day one of his or her training. And why do I claim this one act has criminal intent?

They told no one what they had done.

Something is very wrong.

Government Budgets

Every year in the fall, our two political parties battle it out to create a budget. In recent years, this charade often includes one or both sides threatening a shutdown. Why do I call it a charade? Because well over 50% of what the U.S. Government spends each year is considered a mandatory item and is not negotiated or adjusted. Most of these non-negotiated items are entitlements such as Social Security. Military spending is often negotiated, but when we fight wars, most of those costs aren't included in the budgeting process. The U.S.

Constitution does not include a balanced budget amendment, but many state constitutions do.

The last time the federal government officially had a balanced budget was during Bill Clinton's second term, in the years 1998, 1999, 2000, and 2001.

The Last Hundred Years of American Wars

Time for a little history lesson! World War I began after Archduke Ferdinand was assassinated, which triggered a series of secret alliances in both Europe and America that resulted in four years of trench warfare. After the World War I, the victors declared it was a *war to end all wars* and punished Germany, which planted the seeds of World War II. The victors also began carving up arbitrary boundaries in the Middle East.

After World War II, Germany and Japan were occupied and rebuilt with the Marshall Plan. The American, German, and Japanese people are still friends to this day. The lasting legacy of the Marshall Plan makes it one of the few post-war positive human success stories that includes everyone who participated in combat and, most importantly, everyone's children. The Korean War ended in a stalemate that is still quite tense. We lost the Vietnam War.

With coalition forces by our side, we quickly pushed Iraq out of Kuwait in 1991. That was a decisive win.

After the 9/11 attacks, we retaliated by invading Iraq a second time and overthrew the government led by Saddam Hussein this time. We did not find any weapons of mass destruction, but the war officially lasted from 2003 to 2011, with disputed results.

We have also had military troops fighting in Afghanistan since 2001. The code name for our operations from 2001 to 2014 was Operation Enduring Freedom, and from 2015 to the present, it has been referred to as Operation Freedom's Sentinel. However, I do not believe anyone—in any country—views our military operations in the Middle East during the past twenty years as a success, or that they have improved anyone's lives in the region or created any value or lasting peace.

In my opinion, over the past hundred years, the United States has entered military conflicts with the best of intentions, both morally and ethically. As I see it, we have never attacked or fought to gain conquests, to seek revenge, or to profit, but still … any open-minded debrief strongly suggests that our recent performance has created little human value at an overwhelming human and financial cost.

At times in our history, America has earned a worldwide reputation for being a beacon of hope, peace, and prosperity, but recently, we seem to have fewer friends around the world. Rebuilding trust with our allies and former foes is never easy. General Stanley McCrystal's brilliant book *My Share of the Task* describes leading troops in Afghanistan, and Colonel Kim Olsen's illuminating book *Iraq and Back: Inside the War to Win the Peace* examines the struggles of rebuilding Iraq. The outstanding documentary *The Fog of War*, directed by Errol Morris, highlights the same challenges and mistakes that were made in the Vietnam War.

Military combat is considered to be the pinnacle of stress: there are limited resources and a changing environment and there aren't always good options. Not only that, but the totality of the financial as well as the human costs of combat can last for generations.

Maybe before we send in our troops to "fix" some geopolitical injustice, we should consider what the endgame is. Will the children and grandchildren of two competing societies be civil friends? Or continued combatants? Human history is clear. To secure lasting peace, rebuilding civil trust between two former combatant societies must occur. In most cases, rebuilding civil trust is just as hard, costly, and elusive as winning a war.

Big Risk does repeat itself. Perhaps instead of writing our glorious history in order to convince ourselves we're the Good Guys, maybe we should debrief our actions to get a better grasp of reality, to improve our Situational Awareness, and to *improve our future performance.*

Something seems very wrong.

Chapter Sixteen:

HOW IS TRENCH WARFARE DEMENTIA TRANSMITTED?

"Shallow understanding from people of good will is more frustrating than absolute misunderstanding from people of ill will."

—Dr. Martin Luther King Jr.

COVID-19 has taught me to be cognizant of the myriad ways in which diseases spread. Trench Warfare Dementia is clearly a communicable disease, spreading from one person to another through a variety of means. My observation detects its spread primarily by listening to others via our devices and/or talking directly to one another.

Because of the explosive and exponential growth of data which flows unceasingly from the Internet, each one of us on the planet has the ability and opportunity or faces the temptation to listen to anyone on the planet who has posted a comment. Another by-product of the Internet, posting our thoughts and comments intentionally, surreptitiously, or maliciously, has become a way of life for almost everyone on the planet.

With a few simple clicks, we can instantly find someone to tell us what we want to hear. Most everyone I talk to claims that they "do their own research," but I find this a specious argument. The reality is that since our society is infected with Trench Warfare Dementia, our ubiquitous devices (TVs, phones, and computers) often place us directly into echo chambers.

It seems the message in *every* echo chamber is repeated ad nauseam and is some similar version of the following: we are good, righteous, and hardworking people and *those people* are hateful, ungrateful, and harmful to our families. Most echo chambers also use a moral, ideological, or theological argument to punch up their message. The history of man is clear: having God on your side is one of the most powerful ways to keep the troops loyal and motivated to fight. The fight between good and evil is always justified.

Since the 2016 election, I have had hundreds of conversations—*with both tribes and trenches*—and I have tried to listen carefully to each side. Probably three-quarters of these conversations occurred with people I knew well. Just like my previous experience of monitoring the often bitter in-fighting of union–managements twenty years earlier, at first, all the comments I heard from family, friends, and workmates seemed to reflect a frustrated chaos. Quickly, however, simple, recurring patterns emerged. And finally, just like before, it seemed as if these epic confrontations were being choreographed by an invisible force.

Earlier, when I was describing the differences between my tribe and my wife's tribe, I mentioned the roots of these differences probably originated from our parents. I'm sure our varied belief systems were also influenced by the particular news networks we watched on TV, what newspapers we read, and the people we cultivated and maintained friendships with. As a pilot, ex-military, churchgoing, gun-owning, conservative Republican, I doubt anyone would be surprised to learn that I have watched Fox News for many years. And still today, in every pilot lounge and hotel gym I frequent, Fox News is blaring constantly.

I voted for President Obama the first time he ran for president, but not the second. It was also during President Obama's second term that I stopped watching Fox News. Why? Because every time I turned on that particular channel during this period, President Obama was always 100% wrong. Now, after watching CNN and MSNBC for the past three years, it is President Trump who is always 100% wrong.

But why am I recounting such banalities as the recent conversations I've had with friends, as well as my TV watching habits? Because I believe both of these daily human activities may reveal two key ingredients that transmit the spread of Trench Warfare Dementia and divide our society. I call these two ingredients *labeling* and *loyalty*.

Listen closely to any personal conversation or TV news cast regarding national politics and you will invariably hear a blanket statement that labels 100% of *all those people* in the other tribe or trenches as *bad or substandard*. These labels usually fall into one of three categories: uncaring, threatening, and/or mystifyingly stupid. Of course, when verbalized, the other tribe often views these same all-inclusive comments (labels) as direct attacks. Also, directly stated or inferred from these labels is a call to action. As a rule, we are not bad, uncaring, or stupid people, but we must be resolute and *loyal* to our good and righteous tribe as well as our barking trench commanders, who are valiantly trying to defend our way of life.

Loyalty, however, can be a double-edged sword. Many of us at SWA will continue to be loyal to Herb, Colleen, and Jim for our entire lives, but that does not mean we always agreed with them. I am loyal to my wife and family, but that *certainly* does not mean I always agree with them either. Loyalty can be one of humans' most desirable qualities, but when *we hold on too tightly to any belief*, we can lose our grip on reality, which greatly impairs our keen problem-solving skills and also diminishes our forward focus.

In the cockpit, if I demand my First Officer's loyalty to me above all others, I become a God-like Captain, and I become dangerous … and as a result, everyone onboard could be in peril. To land safely each and every time, I need my First Officer to critically monitor my actions, my words, and my thinking, and for him *to directly challenge me if he or she senses something is awry or that we are headed in the wrong direction.*

In the cockpit, 100% loyalty and/or 100% compliance is a death trap.

The words being hurled around by barking trench commanders are not open-minded observations of reality; they are unyielding closed-minded commendations leading directly to confrontation. These labels and requirements of absolute loyalty preclude any constructive conversations, any self-policing, and/or working together to problem-solve—*even when Big Risk, such as the coronavirus, is attacking our families.*

Even when these statements are stated without any malice by good people, it still only leads to one place. Do you remember my fly-fishing friend? He is one of the finest, helpful, loving, Christian people I know, but he essentially *labeled all Muslims as hateful toward Christians*. I have lived in a Muslim nation and traveled to many others. I am not sure my Christian friend has ever even so much as *talked* to a Muslim.

Remember when I saw recurring patterns emerged and epic confrontations seemed to be choreographed by an invisible force? From my observations, these patterns first emerge from our tendency to begin labeling 100% of *those people*. It's always easier for these patterns to emerge if we do not know each other, or if they do not look like us, or we have not spoken to one another. Once we have labeled people as 100% threatening, then the next step is to feel persecuted or to play the victim. Now the invisible forces of fear and stupidity are free to take hold.

In this situation, our minds are closed. We are not focused forward. We have lost touch with reality and our Situational Awareness skills maybe working against us. We have created alternate realities and must remain absolutely loyal to these realities to survive. Now that our loyalty and these alternate realties have been established, barking trench commanders are free to lead us into battle.

Now that our minds are closed and we feel threatened, *we can easily weaponize God to call us to action*. Now, with these fundamental forces swirling around in our heads, it morally and ethically confirms our complete justification to forcibly repel the forces of evil. This is how Trench Warfare Dementia is transmitted—and how it infects and divides our society

Trench Warfare Dementia creates two warring cults. The barking trench commanders carve out two alternate realities where our entire existence on earth is viewed as black or white, good or evil, or as a blessing from God or sins against God. No effective Situational Awareness skills exist in these worlds. No timely course corrections are made. There is no judgment, only the practice of being judgmental. The only option is compliance.

Dear reader, I want to be crystal clear. From my observations, *both tribes and trenches are infected.* And here is another troubling observation, Trench Warfare Dementia may be a global pandemic. America is not the only nation at war with itself. Around the globe, authoritarian regimes have risen in many democratic countries with market-based economies. This rise in populism is traveling a chaotic path and creating some strange bedfellows along the way. It is also placing power, wealth, and control into the hands of a few belligerent leaders.

The bottom line is that when people around the world divide themselves, can't talk civilly to each other, and hoard their resources from one another, the world we live in becomes a much more dangerous place for ourselves and for our families.

Chapter Seventeen:

TOOLS AND TECHNIQUES DEALING WITH REALITY, LARGE GROUPS, AND EACH OTHER

"During a timeout—especially if things were going badly—Coach K would always say: 'What's the next play?'"

—FORMER DUKE BASKETBALL PLAYER
COMMENTING ON LEGENDARY COACH
MIKE KRZYZEWSKI

There's a saying we have in aviation that perfectly prioritizes every moment of flight: aviate, navigate, and communicate. And when flying an airplane, we do so in that specific order. A Google search of this saying may attribute it to many figures throughout history, but I attribute it to good, old-fashioned aviation wisdom.

This wisdom reminds pilots to always concentrate on *flying the airplane first*. In other words, we must give the airplane our full attention until we are sure it is doing what we intended it to do—*especially when the autopilot is on*! So many pilots have crashed perfectly good airplanes, simply because they got distracted. If the pilot is in control of the airplane (aviating) and it is going in the proper direction (navigating), then, and only then, are the pilots allowed to talk on the radios and communicate.

In an odd twist of reality, this is one of the few times that wisdom from the cockpit does not perfectly fit in dealing with the stress we often face on the ground. The wisdom still holds, but the priority must be reversed. Step one, for most any problem-solving task on the ground, normally includes the ability to talk to one another effectively, *without amplifying the stress or making matters worse*. At the risk of completely oversimplifying things, all we need as a society is to first regain our ability to talk to one another respectfully.

Here is one last piece of aviation wisdom: Flexibility is the key to airpower.

This next story will present several simple lists designed to be helpful tools and technique to deal with reality, large groups, and each other. These are NOT offered as rules to live by. These are NOT procedures or processes promising success or the Promised Land. Complying strictly with these lists does not work, so please feel free to use them in a flexible manner.

Before we get started, I want to remind us that the neurobiologists have discovered that we in fact have two brains. One is lightning fast and is good for fighting or running away (Trench Warfare Dementia). Our other brain is a bit slower but is great for problem-solving (Situational Awareness) and relationships (the Good Guys Team).

Talking to Each Other

1. Talk and listen to each other civilly, constructively, and creatively

2. Relax our tendency to hold on too tightly to the good things in our lives

3. Let go of perceived injustices and things we categorize as "bad"

Just this week, an interaction with one of my neighbors clued me in on how we can still effectively communicate with one another, even when we know we disagree on fundamental issues. The neighbor in question is firmly in my tribe, but he repeatedly and firmly voiced his opinion that it is of vital importance that we respect everyone, no matter what they believe to be true.

While we were talking, he pointed to another neighbor's house and said, "I love the guy who lives in that house. His friendship means everything to me ... but he's a lefty. We both recognize and respect our differences, and because of that, we choose to steer our conversations away from politics, usually with a big smile and lots of laughter."

My neighbor also has three grown kids. One of his daughters is also a lefty (his label). He mentioned that, recently, they kept falling into a series of escalating political conversations, and stubbornly, neither one of them would back down. After a particularly ugly chat with his daughter, they negotiated new ground rules: neither one would be allowed to attack the other by making blanket statements. Also, if either one felt attacked, they were permitted to call their attacker out. After explaining the ground rules, he laughed, "I'll be damned if my daughter wasn't constantly calling me out. And you know? She was often right."

Flexibility is the essence of an open mind. It works in human conversations, too.

I would like to make another observation about my neighbor. He is a salesman. I have noticed that good salespeople do not view the differences in our beliefs system as a reason to feel attacked, to get angry, or to counterattack. Even in today's stressed-out environment, most salespeople I know have a keen sense of humor and know how to time it perfectly with a smile or a self-deprecating joke to smooth over any rough spots in a conversation.

I once complimented a friend, who worked in sales, on her stellar conversational skills. She just smiled and said, "If a salesperson can't hear an objection or a perceived attack and still keep listening, they'll never be successful. Sales is a numbers game. If a salesperson lets rejection upset them, or takes it personally, they will never find the customers they need to thrive."

Hmmm ... and I thought all wisdom originated from the cockpit!

These universal conversational skills from sales professionals are the exact opposite of what I call the "sound-bite, ratcheting, and exploding" conversation. Recently, on a family vacation, I watched a sudden eruption between two people who were solidly in different tribes, but who deeply love each other. In many ways they are each other's caregivers.

It occurred at picnic table and started with light chit-chat. The older member of the two attempted to casually explain something happening in current events using words of his generation. This offended the younger member, who happened to be female. She countered with a widely used "sound-bite" response, which basically labeled him as an uncaring sexist. He momentary tried to explain himself, but his tone was direct, if not angry. She quickly cut him off, armed with more accusations. His words stammered in stunned defense. The entire verbal explosion was over in forty-five seconds when she leapt up from the table and stomped off, leaving the older gentleman speechless.

About an hour later, tensions subsided, the conversation was never discussed again, and the vacation continued. I am guessing that many readers have witnessed, or participated in, similar family experiences.

I hope there are several takeaways from these stories. In today's environment, with data coming at us from everywhere we turn, we shouldn't be surprised that we often bump into strongly held beliefs. In our current society, infected with Trench Warfare Dementia, when we are having any discussion of current events, *we should expect to hear catchy sound bite labels or phrases demanding loyalty.*

These catchy sound bite phrases used by barking trench commanders *are specifically designed to feel threatening*, which keeps everyone in their trenches and energizes both troops to fight each other. If everyone feels like they are being attacked, the barking trench commanders stay in power—and we all lose. When we hear something that feels threatening—and we will—it is instantly a question of which of our two brains we are going to use. If we let our lightning fast, flight or fight brain take charge, we will reinforce and spread Trench Warfare Dementia.

In the same situation, however, if we pause for a moment while continuing to listen to the other person without getting angry, then we can let our problem-solving brain kick in, which will help us keep moving forward. At this moment, if we can channel the wisdom of salespeople, we can head toward building Good Guys Teams.

Trench and Tribe Techniques

This list is for dealing with our own tribe, echo chamber, or trench when we recognize that it is more harmful to be hunkered down and isolated than it is to be working with others who we may not always agree with or look like. In these situations, we need to ask ourselves one pertinent question: Do we welcome diversity or do we fear it?

The purpose of these tools and techniques is two-old. First, they work to loosen the power our tribe holds over each of us. And second, these techniques help make our tribe less combative and abusive toward those we perceive as "other." In order to work well together and put our differences aside, we must:

1. Talk, listen, and ask questions of each other

2. Withhold enthusiasm—Do not cheer for the barking trench commanders

3. Self-police when hearing bullshit or hatred or nearing danger

Using these tools and techniques can be awkward, so I suggest trying them out gently at first, as suddenly taking a decisive stand usually just results in falling on your sword, which benefits no one. The general rule of thumb is to not cheer or repeat the catchy sound bite phrases used by the barking trench commanders. When the roar of the crowd subsides, quietly ask pointed questions about consequences, such as how much will this cost us? What are the unintended consequences of these actions? And based on these current actions, who will we become?

Listen intently to any responses without feeling the need to agree or judge. There is no need to get into a heated debate. Sometimes a calm, inquisitive response eventually speaks loudly.

PART FIVE: DEBRIEF TO IMPROVE FUTURE PERFORMANCE

Chapter Eighteen:

FAMILY FIRST CITIZENSHIP MODEL—MY WIFE'S TRIBE

"Ask not what your country can do for you, ask what you can do for your country"

—JFK's Inauguration Speech, 1961

Make no mistake about it. It is more crucial than ever to yank ourselves out of Trench Warfare Dementia, hack off selective, strident alternate reality viewpoints that have been placed in our heads by barking trench commanders, and push us back to the middle, where we can problem-solve together. Most importantly, *we need to rebuild the Good Guys Team, with two out of three of us sharing the same mental model.* What we are doing now is not fun or helpful. It creates divisiveness and is exhausting and dangerous—especially to our children.

The Family First Citizenship Model is my attempt to corral my wife's tribe's expectations of what goods and services our government should actually be responsible for providing to its citizens. However, since my roots *do not* come from this tribe—*and I want to stay happily married*—this will be the kinder, gentler analysis of the two. Rest assured that in the following chapter, I will self-police my own tribe with significantly more energy.

My use of the common term, Good Guys, originated twenty years ago when I was predicting labor votes. The strident groups on both edges were called Kool-Aid Drinkers (who believed that the boss was 100% right) and the Bolsheviks (who believed that the boss was 100% wrong). In normal times, both edge groups only made up around 10% of the entire group, and the Good Guys were in the middle, occupying around two-thirds of the group. But in stressful times, the membership percentages of each group changed. In extended periods of extreme stress, the ranks of the Bolsheviks swelled and trenches began to form. Many Bolsheviks became barking trench commanders.

In less stressful times, the Good Guys made up the majority of the entire group. Earlier, I noticed that when any large group gets to the point where two out of three of the members are working well together (singing from the same sheet of music or have a shared mental model), then something magical happens. It's a tipping point and as a result, they can now become a powerful team who regularly perform the following tasks:

1. Talk and listen to each other

2. Problem-solve together

3. Make timely course corrections

Since civilizations began forming along the rivers in the Middle East over five thousand years ago, there has always been a nature tension between raising a family, making money as a worker or owner, and how the large group is ruled, organized, or governed. Today it is no different.

While all three components play a vital role, I strongly believe the quality of our families is the foundation and engine of any society or civilization. (Please recall my previous disclaimer, as I encourage the reader to use their own definition of family.)

Earlier, when I described being the boss of a business, I also used a family analogy. The boss must raise and nurture three kids: the consumer, workers, and profit-motive child. All three of these kids are raising their own families, but the reality is the consumer and the worker are the same person raising the same family. If the consumer and worker families joined forces, they could become an incredible, powerful, we-the-people team.

Also noted earlier, in a democratic, capitalistic society, each of these families technically has three powerful votes: voting at the ballot box, buying things and creating demand, and what's in our heads. Since it's generally assumed that our economy is driven by consumer spending, if we collectively use our three votes wisely, then we should be able to control our future, or at least strongly influence it.

Unfortunately however, when the society is infected with Trench Warfare dementia, we divide our limited resources and outsource our three votes to barking trench commanders *on both sides*, and therefore, wash all our money first through hidden corridors of crony capitalism. Our families? Well, they are left with table scraps, and no one likes to be manipulated or manhandled or to see their families suffer.

Which leads me to a few critiques of my wife's tribe: Believing our government should provide a full spectrum of good and services to help each American family without asking the questions how we are going to pay for it and who's going to pay for it? (This is similar emotional denial logic my tribe uses to justify fighting wars.) Both thought processes conveniently ignore all the unfunded liabilities and promises already made by the U.S. Congress. And last, but certainly not least, creating and reinforcing print and TV media that tells this tribe only what they want to hear.

Part of these critiques points out the glaring fact that the U.S. consumer has sure screwed the hell out of the U.S. worker! Please explain to me why the American worker self-righteously complains about job losses to overseas workers, *but the same person ravenously buys the lowest-priced products made overseas?* If we continue to buy the lowest-priced products, then more than likely that the lowest-priced worker will get the job. If a "made in USA" tag on a product means nothing to the U.S. consumer, then why should it mean anything to a U.S. business?

If we Americans bought more products made in America, there would be more jobs in the United States as well. When it comes to food items, is the U.S. consumer making healthy choices? When it comes to environmental costs or pollution, is the U.S. consumer demanding healthy choices?

The demand we create matters. The ultimate costs and consequences of the demand we create matter too.

The third critique of my wife's tribe centers on the media that we both watch together almost every night. We receive a copy of *The New York Times* daily newspaper and normally watch CNN or MSNBC. On the whole, I think all three have a coterie of outstanding professional journalists reporting from their ranks. My critique, however, is twofold. First, the White House and the other tribe are always 100% wrong. While I normally agree with their reasoning and commentary, the world is not black and white. Neither side is universally wrong or unfailingly right.

Second, these three media outlets never seem to delve into the most vexing political question of the day. Despite odd, despicable, and/or dangerous behavior and comments from the White House, why does such a consistently high percentage of Americans still support the President? It seems CNN or MSNBC gets giddy if they can find a poll showing the President's support has fallen from 42% to 38%. However, my question is, how can 38% of the Americans still be supporting him at all? If these media outlets wanted to report on both sides, Democrats and Republican, I would think they would feel obligated to find the answer to this pertinent question.

In conclusion, I developed the Family First Citizenship Model from listening to stories from combat on the battlefield. Time and time again I've heard soldiers on the front lines say that yes, they believe or hope that the country and their generals were doing the right thing, but their primary concern was *taking care of themselves and their buddies fighting next them*. When bullets are flying, these soldiers aren't fighting for America or democracy or freeing an oppressed people, they are fighting to survive and taking care of those immediate around them.

As a grateful nation, we should never ask any more of our soldiers. As a grateful nation, I don't think we should ask any more of our working American families. Yes, each person and their family have responsibilities to be good citizens, but their primary energy and focus should be to take good care of their families and others who may be nearby.

Here is a list of three edicts (with a few modifications) which have the potential to merge healthy families with healthy citizenship:

1. Talk to, listen, and support one another.

2. Share challenges, hold yourself responsible for your actions, and withhold enthusiasm for bad behavior within the family.

3. Self-police errant behavior within the family, so local police do not have to intervene and/or governments do not have to add support.

When families are healthy, pride in citizenship can emerge and a powerful Goods Guys Team will carry everyone forward. When two out of three working families are in good hands, then America has a firm foundation, a powerful engine, and a sense of keen Situational Awareness that can thrive, and as a result, the fifty states of the union become united once again.

God bless, the *United States of America*.

Chapter Nineteen:

ME AND MY TRIBE

*"All suffering is caused by ignorance. People inflict
pain on others in the selfish pursuit of their own
happiness or satisfaction."*

—Dalai Lama

From earlier discussions of large-group dynamics, I noted that it is
the *responsibility of members within the group to self-police* errant
or evil behavior (words or deeds) from percolating or leading the
group astray. I previously described myself, as well as my tribe as,
"often made up pilots, ex-military, Texans, churchgoing Christians
and gun owners. All these characteristics are naturally who I am,
and for most of my life, I have voted as a fiscally responsible, conservative Republican." Let's start my in-house discussion with the set of
similar critiques I made of my wife's tribe. In doing so, I have merely
changed a few words.

First, my tribe generally believes that our government should
provide a full spectrum of goods and services to help each *corporation*.

My tribe is also in denial of the U.S. debt load created by the governmental goods and services currently being provided and ignores all the unfunded liabilities and promises already made by the Congress.

My tribe often creates a dysfunctional, harmful demand that creates little or no value for hardworking families.

My tribe has created, and religiously funded, media outlets that tell us exactly what we want to hear.

Self-Policing in Pilot Speak

Since when did my tribe—some of the hardest working Americans, some of the most morally "stand-up"-type leaders, and people that work tirelessly for their families—suddenly become God-like Captains? In other words, authoritative, dangerous assholes who won't listen to anyone! Since when did we become so angry, fearful, and hateful in stressful situations?

We used to be trusted leaders under stress. We used to teach Situational Awareness skills and daily demonstrate Yankee flexibility and ingenuity. We were the Good Guys who could always find a sustainable path forward. When the going got tough, we were the ones everyone turned to in order to make safe landings. We took great pride in our unwavering ability to take care of ourselves, our families, and each other.

So why have we now become so fucking stupid?

Since when did my tribe start cheering dystopian leaders with dog whistles who just make shit up every day?

Military Bearing

This story speaks to my core values and those of my closest and most respected, ex-military friends, many who are also gun owners like me. When I was in the military, we were expected to follow orders and work together as a team. We were trained to use our Situational Awareness skills to get the job done properly—the first time. We were drilled—and constantly reminded—*to never become complacent* about accomplishing simple or complex tasks, while always keeping a vigilant eye out for danger.

Most importantly, we were taught how to follow orders and also to take care of each other at the same time. Naturally, these twin, fundamental mission directives occasionally collided, and we (the troops) were expected to deal with reality. Specifically, I am talking about when the orders from the commander defied common sense or did not reasonably fit the task demanded of us.

If the commander was respected but his orders missed the mark, I often saw another senior officer quietly go into his office and close the door. Everyone in the squadron understood what self-policing message was being delivered behind that door. However, if the commander was not respected and/or was just trying to bullshit his way through a briefing, the group sat quietly … and simply ignored his words.

My point here is, despite the highly structured command of the U.S. military, the troops were NOT trained to be brainwashed, Kool-Aid Drinkers or sycophants. We knew instinctively that blindly following bullshit orders would make the entire group complacent, which could lead to danger. Yes, military command authority is assigned, but respect for leadership must be earned.

On January 20, 2017, Donald Trump became the Commander-in-Chief of the U.S. military. Within hours of him taking the oath to "preserve, protect and defend the Constitution of the United States," he initiated a bizarre public food fight that his inauguration crowd was larger than Barack Obama's. It was bullshit and everyone knew it. And at this exact moment, every man and women ever trained with military bearing—or common sense—should have raised the bullshit flag.

After all, were we taught to blindly follow authority figures who have clearly lost touch with reality or who routinely lie? Were we brainwashed to follow leaders who were more concerned about their own image than the success of the mission? Were we encouraged to be sycophants to commanders who incessantly bragged, while spewing hate for others in our own command?

That's not how I was taught military bearing.

This was not an isolated incident; it became the new American Presidential normal. It became a daily tweet storm of the President viciously attacking anyone and everyone. He quickly called America's free press "fake news," dog-whistled a league of White supremacists in a call to action, said global warming was a hoax, and projected "deep state" messaging designed to make every America's institutions to bow down to his every whim.

Whenever the cameras were rolling, he was actively lying.

Even after all that, three and a half years later, many of my ex-military First Officers and friends are still staunch Trump supporters. Crowds still gather and enthusiastically cheer him. Let me be clear, I believe this continued support for a person *clearly unfit for duty* is taking America down a path—coupled with our bulging debt—from which we may never recover.

A National Disgrace in Decision-Making

I first started hearing about the rising costs of health care from Herb Kelleher in the early 1990s. One night, as I was enjoying dinner with Herb and Colleen, we discussed my plans to join a start-up, family home-building business. After listening for a moment, Herb briefly commented, "Watch out for health-care benefits for employees. At the airline, we're seeing double-digit cost increases each year."

The next time I recall hearing about health-care costs was during Bill Clinton's presidency, when he appointed his wife, Hillary Clinton, to tackle the national problem. Her efforts were dead-on-arrival, but I still recall hearing many self-righteous, congratulatory comments from my tribe members. Things like, "There's no way that liberal bitch is going to tell us how to run our country!"

Over the years in between, I did not pay keen attention to health-care costs, as I had come from the military with full medical benefits, and now worked for an airline with excellent union-negotiated benefits. My family's coverage was good, and our costs were reasonable. I do recall, however, being somewhat mystified by medical billing. When my daughter was involved in a small traffic accident as a passenger, bumping her head against the windshield, she spent four hours in the local ER. All the tests run proved negative and she was fine. However, six weeks later, I reviewed the medical charges. The ER charged the insurance company $6,500 for four hours of work and tests. The insurance negotiated the bill down to $2,500, and I ended up paying $400.

My question is, who's the poor schmuck who has to pay $6,500?

Later, while still employed at the airline, I joined a small asset management firm. It was a one-man shop and I became number two. My partner's annual medical insurance costs, for both him and his wife, were $18,000, and that included a $5,000 deductible for each of them! By this time, it should have been obvious to every leader in this country that rising medical costs were pounding the crap out of American families—especially families who didn't happen to work for corporations.

And then came the Affordable Care Act (ACA), or Obama Care, which was passed in 2010, when the Democrats controlled all three branches of government. Essentially, no Republicans from my tribe voted in favor of it. And ever since 2010, every member of my tribe has viciously bad-mouthed its existence as destroying the very fabric of America. Every one of our barking trench commanders has made it a rallying cry to rid ourselves of this pestilence. During this time, every candidate from my tribe pledged to defeat it.

But in 2016, the ideological crusade reached the Promised Land and the Republicans regained control of all three branches. Now they were in charge, and the Obama Care curse on America would soon be gone!

I chuckle when history repeats itself. Campaign promises and rhetoric often get revised after winning. Instantly my tribe started touting they were going to improve the ACA and that after this reform, "it would be beautiful, with coverage for everyone at even lower costs." I remember the Speaker of the House, Paul Ryan, the day before they tried to pass new ACA legislation effectively saying, "We (Republicans) have been working on improving Obamacare for seven years, and we need to pass these improvements for American families."

Reflecting the devastating impacts of being a divided country, no meaningful improvements have occurred. After twenty-five years of elected leaders bickering like adolescent teenagers, medical costs and a lack of coverage are still threatening American families. Over twenty-five years ago, my wife's tribe first recognized the reality of limited or nonexistent medical care for American families and its subsequent impact on American families. Since then, my tribe has lived in an alternate reality of crony capitalism and protected corporations.

I am not saying that the ACA is perfect, or even that it works well. But it certainly was a much-needed course correction away from Big Risk for American families. If during the past twenty-five years, two out of three of us had been working together on the Good Guys Team with keen Situational Awareness skills, we could have been continuously debriefing the ACA in order to improve our future performance.

Instead, twenty-five years after my tribe cheered and called Hillary Clinton a liberal bitch, we still have the highest medical costs in the world, and coverage that literally punishes many American families.

Now, that's a national disgrace in decision-making.

God, Masks, and Hypocrites

Last year, I was having coffee with one of my closest friends. Our conversations are usually a combination of faith and politics, and in discussing both in tandem, we often butt heads. His faith is more firmly rooted in the evangelical camp, and I often get the feeling he considers my Presbyterian faith as spiritually deficient. Unsurprisingly, I was yakking away about how close our society was to Big Risk and how fearful I was that God might decide to "restructure." He got a huge smile on his face, raised his arms up, and bellowed, "And it would be glorious!" I told him he was crazy, but he just kept on smiling.

I told him I was God-fearing and reminded him about Noah, his ark, and worldwide flooding. But my friend was undeterred. He proclaimed that God had a plan for all us and that he and he alone completely controlled life on earth. God protects his true believers, he informed me, and if God decided to start over again, he would welcome it. We had been down this path before, he and I. So without reacting verbally, I simply shook my head in disgust and changed the subject to football.

As I have stated many times before, I have no desire and no need to change anyone's personal belief system. I do, however, never hesitate to throw the bullshit flag when they project the consequences of their beliefs on my family and onto others. Also, I do not believe the sole responsibility for protecting me and my family rests exclusively on God's to-do list.

After all, wasn't America created on the foundational belief of the separation of church and state?

I'd like to stop here and suggest that I may be misrepresenting the character of my friend. He is a devoted father and husband. He takes great care of his family and is a successful businessman. Still, I bristle at the idea that God has theoretically given him a special coat of armor because of his beliefs. Bad things *do* happen to good people.

As I am writing this story, deaths as a result of COVID-19 are approaching the 130,000 mark, and America is opening back up. On Facebook, I saw a post from another one of my evangelical Christian friends, saying she was refusing to wear a mask because she believed that God was protecting her. But since when did our belief in a higher power give us the right to disregard science? Global warming is now a hoax, just because we are true believers? The chosen ones? Since when did wearing a mask during a global pandemic become a statement about God's power or a political fight for liberty?

My own faith began to grow exponentially later in life, but it gives me great comfort and helps me navigate life wisely. I feel that reading the scriptures not only keeps me grounded and enhances my situational awareness but also holds me responsible for my words and deeds. It reminds me that I am responsible for the consequences of my actions, too.

I read from a NIV Bible. The first three topics in Matthew VI talk about giving to the needy, prayer, and fasting. The word the NIV version uses for people bragging about their beliefs is "hypocrite." And speaking of hypocrites, I often feel like one when I attend church. While attending church each week, I am reminded by our pastors to confess my sins and that my sins are forgiven by God. As I see it, sins are seriously bad deeds, words, or thoughts, not the kind of banal, stupid, everyday mistakes I routinely commit.

I also know that I must recognize and debrief my failures to improve my future performance. Each week at church, I assume the sermon I am listening to will help me walk closer to God. But if this true then what did I learn from previous sermons? Am I really taking responsibility for my actions? Or improving my future performance? Or am I just being a hypocrite?

Also, why have so many conservative, evangelical Christian churches put an unyielding flag in the ground over the very societal issues that divide us? Was that Jesus' message for us? Divide and conquer? Why do some our most vitriolic and influential barking trench commanders come from the pulpit? Instead of weaponizing God, why can't Christians embrace the Bible as a personal problem-solving tool to help us wisely navigate life on earth and take better care of each other?

I'd like to ask all of the "true believers" who proudly trumpet their beliefs and ferociously hold tightly to them, who did Jesus have trouble with? And who helped nailed him to the cross? It was the Pharisees, Sadducees, and the temple money changers (bankers). All three were supremely confident that only they understood and believed the correct interpretation of the laws of the Old Testament. Worldwide, many in my tribe like to publicly talk a lot of "Christian smack," especially to the other children of our Father Abraham. However, my personal reading of the Bible suggests we should walk more humbly and demonstrate significantly more empathy for others.

Perhaps, God believes that all the humans on earth are his children—not just the chosen ones sitting in our respective pews.

A Football Player Takes a Knee

As I previously mentioned, I have a military background and proudly wear an American flag tie around my neck while flying for

Southwest. I strongly believe in what the American flag stands for, and I hold on tightly to this belief … maybe a little too tightly.

A few years ago, I was watching a National Football League game when several Black football players began kneeling during the national anthem. The ringleader, Colin Kaepernick, was a quarterback who at the time probably made over a million dollars a game. As I sat there and watched, I grew increasingly agitated. *Really? I* thought. *Can't I watch a frigging football game without being subjected to some spoiled, rich athlete whining about his hardships and perceived injustice. Didn't we just elect a Black President twice—you ungrateful bastards!* However, immediately after the kickoff, I completely forgot about the incident.

But several days later, while at work with my guys friends (all White), it was clear that the episode was far from forgotten. Sports media lit up like a Christmas tree. Again, I did not comment, I just sat there and listened to my colleagues, my friends, and the media. And what I heard was more than ugly, it was downright vitriolic and hateful. I don't think I heard the N-word used, but the sentiment and anger I did hear was nauseating enough.

This response from friends, the media, and my trusted colleagues caused me to stop, think, and reflect. I wrestled with my thoughts, observations, and assessments for several days and came to this realization. Kaepernick took a knee. He didn't give the finger to the national anthem. He didn't say, "All you frigging White guys need to go back to where you came from." On the football field, taking a knee is not considered an aggressive move with malicious intent. It's a respectful way to stop the game for one play.

As the furor escalated over a few more Black NFL athletes protesting before their games, CNN held a town hall meeting on air anchored by Anderson Cooper. This is a partial transcript of that show where NFL player, then Philadelphia Eagles safety, Malcolm Jenkins was interviewed. For those who are unaware, Cooper is White, and Jenkins is Black. Their conversation begins:

COOPER: Malcom, thanks so much for being with us, I appreciate it.

JENKINS: Thanks for having me.

COOPER: You said this is not a new protest. You've been, since last season, raising a fist during the national anthem. And I wondered if you could just explain why.

JENKINS: Well, one thing that I think that's been missing this entire year is us getting to the real issues. I think it started when, last summer, you had the shooting of Philando Castile and Alton Sterling. And as a Black man in America with a platform, I no longer wanted to stand behind social media while we posted hashtag after hashtag of Black people dying at the hands, unnecessarily, of law enforcement.

And so the first thing I wanted to do was get an understanding of how I could play a role in becoming part of the solution. And the way I did that was sitting down with local police officers and finding out what some of their struggles were, their issues were, their training, did they need resources? And through those conversations, we began to work on some dialogue and how we could better that relationship.

And soon thereafter you had the protest of Colin Kaepernick and I think what that did was that it showed athletes who are doing this work behind the scenes, that we could bring this stuff to the forefront and really change the dialogue nationally about these issues and drawn attention to what's happening in our communities.

COOPER: And Malcom, to those who say taking a knee during the national anthem, or not coming out during the national anthem, is disrespectful, it's unpatriotic, disrespectful to the flag, what do you say?

JENKINS: I could understand where that could come from and why they would feel that way. But I think you have to check the track record of a lot of players that are demonstrating and the NFL in general. I think we do a great job of honoring our military, our flag through our events. We have first responders, military, and police at almost every NFL game that we honor and hold up high. But this is not about them, it's not about our flag at all, this is us, as concerned citizens, trying to play our role in a bigger conversation about race in America, a bigger conversation about our criminal justice system, and our law enforcement. And this is not an indictment against law enforcement or police. We're not anti-police. Many of us have worked hand-in-hand with law enforcement to figure out ways to really move us forward in a better direction. To re-instill trust in our law enforcement and to really hold that accountability and transparency that our communities are looking for.

(End of transcript.)

Regrettably, I do not think anyone in the White community even recalls Jenkins' words of wisdom today. The entire thesis of this book is that we, as a society, desperately need to collectively move from continuously fighting each other to problem-solving together. In rereading the words of Malcom Jenkins, *I don't think I can a find a better example of the power and brilliance of a problem-solving mind-set, while respectfully addressing one of the toughest issues that divides our society.*

Sadly, as I am in the process of completing this book on May 31, 2020, there is protest and violence in the streets of American over the lynching of George Floyd. I firmly believe that if America had taken the opportunity to embrace the deeds and words of two Black, NFL football players back in 2016, we would be in a much better place today.

Trench Warfare Dementia: Hate, Dog Whistles, and Evil

Earlier when I discussed group dynamics of the Good Guys model, I stated that the strident groups, Kool-Aid Drinkers and Bolsheviks, each only made up 10% to 15% of the entire group. This leaves two out of three of us Good Guys in the middle to steer the ship and carry the load.

Previously, I fondly labeled the Bolsheviks as "odd ducks" with excellent radars. As I mentioned, I rarely agreed with the Bolsheviks, but I always learned something interesting when I talked to them— and many ended up becoming good friends. The larger group of Good Guys, however, often looked down upon Bolsheviks with disdain, or worse, hatred. I believe, from a large-group security point of view, this to be a tactical error.

Here is a little wisdom which is attributed to the original inhabitants of America. An old Cherokee told his grandson, "My son, there is a battle between two wolves inside us all. One is Evil. It is anger, jealousy, greed, resentment, inferiority, lies, and ego. The other is Good. It is joy, peace, love, hope, humility, kindness, empathy, and truth."

The boy thought about it and asked: "Grandfather, which wolf wins?"

The old man quietly replied, "The one you feed."

In truth, there is always a small element of evil that exists within any large group. The reality of the matter is that a tiny bit of evil lives in all humans. Self-respect, self-discipline, and having empathy for others, however, mean that the seed of evil does not get fed. When Bolsheviks are treated with respect, they can provide the larger group its most powerful self-policing, safety net early, not to mention early warnings against impending evil. But when Bolsheviks are demonized, none of this occurs. When the greater society reflects a Good Guys Team, then only a tiny percentage of evil is nurtured, usually emerging from troubled souls. Where will tiny element of evil gravitate toward? Not the Kool-Aid Drinkers or the Good Guys; it seeks hidden cover in the Bolshevik territory.

Think about it. If the Bolsheviks are warmly tolerated with a smile by the larger group, they will be the first to detect evil brewing. If the Bolsheviks have not been isolated by the larger group, they will naturally protect the larger group by self-policing and appropriately alerting the group before any harm can occur.

But if the Bolsheviks are isolated or demonized by the larger group, they will feel zero obligation to alert anyone. Even when the Good Guys model is somewhat intact, if we stop talking to each other, isolate or demonize each other, we reflect hate. The dangerous reality of this path, however, is we also unknowingly hide, grow, and nurture evil. A divided society infected with Trench Warfare Dementia does not nurture evil, it emboldens evil. The reckless and dangerous acts of our leaders who publicly spew hatred can also legitimize evil.

Thanks to the NRA convincing my tribe that our Black, Democratic President wanted to take all our guns and that we needed military weaponry to defend ourselves against a tyrannical, deep-state government, now any potential home-ground person, with evil swirling around in their head, has easy access to plenty of firepower.

If the NRA actually took gun safety seriously, they should have been demanding proper training and licensing all along. Instead, the NRA's reckless and dangerous acts, backstopped by every Republican senator, have condemned the American society to random acts of evil and violence against all our families for many generations.

Isolating, demonizing, and hating others is a human boomerang. These thoughts, words, and deeds may feel comforting to some fearful souls, but in reality, it functions as the world's dumbest security blanket. And as a result, these ugly acts can now unleash evil on any American family, without warning.

Chapter Twenty:

BIG RISK DEBRIEFS

"Even if you are on the right track, you will get run over if you just sit there."

—WILL ROGERS

I started writing this book foolishly believing that the Boeing Max airplane crashes would be the top example of Big Risk in this country. However, since then, as a divided nation we have faced COVID-19, and now another police killing of a Black man with countrywide protests as a result.

Boeing airplanes and the U.S. FAA used to represent the worldwide gold standard in aviation. Now American aviation represents another dangerous example of capitalism run amok. Following the maximizing shareholder value playbook and a relentless persecution of profits, Boeing executives overrode the years of trust previously earned by building reliable airplanes with triple redundancy primary systems. Worse than designing an unsafe airplane, Boeing purposely hid their unthinkable behavior from regulators, airlines, and pilots.

No Boeing executive, or its Board of Directors, wanted their airplanes to crash. Still the reality is that their relentless pressure on the organization to "make their quarterly numbers" makes them directly responsible for institutionalizing the bad behavior that has opened the ugly and evil doors causing the crashes.

In my opinion, this is criminal behavior. *To send a clear message to other corporations* that this type of institutional bad behavior needs to be eradicated from the way America does business, I would seek criminal indictments and five-to-ten-year prison terms for each Boeing executive *and the entire Board of Directors*.

When dangerous institutionalized bad behavior or criminal leadership behavior exists, those responsible need to be reminded what *skin in both games* means. This simple notion is how pilots have earned the trust of passengers over the course of many years. This same simple notion can help America's highest-paid corporate executives regain our trust.

COVID-19

As of today, the COVID-19 pandemic has killed 400,000 people worldwide and over 130,000 in the United States. Every day there are raging debates in the media regarding the ways in which we are handing this pandemic and what should be done about it. I know several people who have been infected, and one member of our church was on a ventilator for a month and barely survived. He returned home yesterday but has a long road to recovery ahead of him.

I have no medical credentials sufficient enough to weigh in on how we should proceed, but even so, I think we can all agree on four things. First, we face this pandemic as a divided society, which significantly weakens and disrupts our national response. Second, global Big Risk issues such as COVID-19 make us realize—or *should* make us realize—that we are all in this together. Third, when facing medical issues (COVID-19) or science issues (global warming), we-the-people need to base our group decision making on accepted wisdom from our doctors, scientists and other professionals, rather than tightly held ideology or theology from snollygosters. For a society to land safely every time, lust for power, greed and crony capitalism should never trump good science, common sense or the greater good. And finally, we increase our chances of survival, recovery, and prosperity if we talk and listen to one another with smiles on our faces and genuine empathy in our hearts.

Police Murder in Minneapolis

I started this book by addressing Big Risk and urging us all to recognizing it early and turning away from it. But when George Floyd's murder was recorded for all to see, it was too late to turn away. America became cracked open with historically raw emotions, yet again. Now it is a game of armed survival, as we continually fight with ourselves.

I have already mentioned that several years ago, Fox News began criticizing President Obama on a seemingly unending loop. I have also mentioned that back in 2016, a Black football player took a knee and the White sports world proceeded to go apoplectic. I mentioned how the U.S. military deals with death, destruction, and institutionalized bad behavior emanating from failed leadership. The reality is racism in America has forcibly been hidden in a closet for our entire history. Now, matters are worse. It's being proudly projected as a "law and order" power play from the top.

This armed conflict has been brewing and its deep roots were cultivated when the conservative media felt the need to endlessly criticize our first Black President while White America either cheered or was silent. The inflection point, or point of no return, may have occurred when America's self-righteous, White sports audience manufactured the narrative that taking a knee was akin to disrespecting the American flag. This crucial, hateful error justified White America's response to ignore any genuine pleas to listen, help, or problem-solve issues of racism, which the White community was responsible for creating over four hundred years ago.

But make no mistake, our fate was cemented when our current Commander-in-Chief gave the order to dominate, demanding law and order and describing our cities as "battle-space" for the U.S. military. These were not veiled threats or dog whistles but direct marching orders from the American President to inflict harm by the U.S. military on the American people.

General Mattis's brilliantly direct and forceful response, published in the Atlantic magazine on June 3, 2020, says it clearly. During World War II, the Nazis' strategy against Allied Forces was to divide and conquer. Make no mistake—this is the exact same strategy President Trump is using against all Americans at this very moment in time.

I do not believe Americans are inherently racist, but one of the consequences of being a divided society is that we are certainly traveling along that path. We have much work ahead of us to repair the damage we have inflicted on ourselves and others. Racism is taught and learned. It can be unlearned, too. But as Steven Covey reminds us, first things, first.

This November we need to remove the evil at the top.

Chapter Twenty-One:

MAJOR COURSE CORRECTIONS

"Sunlight is the best disinfectant."

—Louis Brandeis

I began *Safe Landings* with an explanation of the Big Risk Doctrine, which stated that we need to recognize Big Risk when it is on the horizon so we can make timely course corrections, turning away before it overwhelms us or our children. Next, I discussed our keen Situational Awareness problem-solving skills and the components of stress: limited resources, changing environments, and not always having good options. Then I delved into the consequences of Trench Warfare Dementia, which divides our resources and propels us to continuously fight one another. When I discussed rebuilding the Good Guys Team, I mentioned that step one was being able to talk to each other. I also noted that the hurdles to rebuilding were complexity, chaos, and the constant feeling of being inundated by overwhelming amounts of data.

Throughout this journey, I tried to steadfastly debrief to improve future performance but not play the blame game. The following list of course corrections are not made as recommendations but rather as a demonstration of possible opportunities we could enact, if we have the will to do so.

Specifically, I did not try to soak the rich to pay for our sins. We are all in this together. I believe if we ask the wealthy to pay more than one out of four dollars earned in federal taxes, then we have bypassed capitalism and are moving toward socialism. I believe that we need to restructure our democratic and capitalism systems, not discard them. However, I did suggest mandatory criminal sentences for reckless and dangerous corporate behavior. These are not offered as a promise to cure the current ills of our society—or to make life more equitable. The only purpose of this list is to give us a clearer picture of reality and to rid ourselves of institutionalized bad behavior.

With a clearer picture, hopefully, we will realize the need to work together, and we will begin to start turning away from Big Risk. When facing large challenges, we will always face a mental fork in the road: Are we seeking a firmer grasp of reality? Or are we going to wiggle out our responsibilities through denial?

I offer this list without further explanation or details, but I believe the intent and the purpose are clear.

1. Twelve-year term limits for total service in Congress. After twelve years of any combination of service in either the Senate or House, a person cannot seek any federal reelection. Similarly, after service in Congress, a person cannot become a federal registered lobbyist. All tax

returns of Congressional members and registered lobbyists must become public record.

2. Term limits for federally appointed judges, and their tax returns must become public record as well.

3. The Electoral College must be eliminated, and all federal elections limited to ninety days—from filing to elections.

4. The U.S. tax code must be abolished and replaced with a flat tax with three levels: 10% 15%, and 20% for both all people and all businesses. There will be no deductions. Everyone pays—no exceptions. Estate taxes must be abolished as well. There will be no upper limits on payroll taxes until Social Security and Medicare become solvent again. Keep nonprofit organizations intact, but make them publicly accountable to be working toward the greater good of *all* citizens..

5. The Glass–Steagall Act for banking, investing, and insurance must be reinstated immediately.

6. We must make corporate "reckless and dangerous" behavior a criminal offense with minimum prison sentences for CEO, CFO, and all members of any Board of Directors.

7. We must eliminate gerrymandering for voting districts and school districts. All voting districts and school districts must align themselves with existing city, county, or state geographic and governmental boundaries.

8. The U.S. military must be restructured with two new primary missions: worldwide disaster relief and domestic

skills training. We should consider making two-year mandatory military service for all young adults.

9. We should require private universities with large endowment funds to create and run domestic businesses, and all private universities must provide direct teaching support and educational resources for local community colleges.

10. We must encourage local churches and faiths to work together, share resources, and participate more directly in local family support, shelter, and feeding opportunities.

11. Communities must repair their relationships with teachers and police. Trust and support—both ways—are vital for any healthy community. School districts and police departments are often too parochial and insular. Instead we must create centralized federally operated training facilities and campuses for both educators as well as police to continuously share best practices, understand their challenges, and evolve their skills. These federally operated training facilities could be placed on college campuses, similar to Reserve Officers' Training Corps (ROTC) facilities. We should create six-week on-site courses at these training facilities and encourage that at least 25% of local teachers and our police will be effectively trained within five years.

12. We must allow states to independently rule on our most divisive issues. Give state legislatures more flexibility to control the goods and services they provide, and let states compete for citizens.

13. We must rejoin the Paris Climate Treaty.

14. All federal regulators should be governed by a five-person voting board where each member will serve for five years. No more than two members at any time can have previous industry experience. After serving, all board members are prohibited for an additional five years from being directly, or indirectly, employed by the industry.

15. Annually, the U.S. Congress must report on all expenses authorized, paid, unfunded liabilities and all debt obligations. Also all expenditures must include a brief statement of purpose and evaluation of what value to American families has been created. Each year, on a rotational basis, select several accounting agencies to independently report to the American people on the abovementioned expenses, liabilities, debt, and value created. Each accounting agency may create both a ten-page and a hundred-page report at their discretion. Each year a public forum will be held to determine which report styles are the most illuminating and helpful to the American voter and taxpayer in understanding both our financial situation and our future.

16. All Congressional legislation will be limited to four thousand words and must include sections describing purpose, intent, examples, costs, and funding. Before voting, the final legislation must be publicly posted, and all members must be given three days to read it or sign documentation that they have read it. No Congressional member or federal employee shall be exempt from the any legislation or regulatory coverage—including the President.

17. We should encourage tech companies to create social media platforms, financed by subscriptions only. No advertising. No bots. Everyone signs their name. There will be no algorithms determining what is viewed or deleted. All posts will be verified as authentic by the tech company, and each tech company is responsible for resolving any issues with hacking.

Chapter Twenty-Two:

TIME TO GO BOOM

"Knowing what must be done does away with fear."

—Rosa Parks

Throughout this book, I have tried to emphasize the concept that we are all in this together, and that our families "have skin in both games." The book has also focused on the large-group dynamics I experienced from failed union–management relationships—specifically elections. My research confirms elections are important, but the numerical results do not always yield the implied results.

As a reminder, it's not until two out of three people vote favorably, or basically agree on the chosen path, that the group gains the potential to become a powerful team, one that is consistently able to move forward safely. If the vote is inside 52% to 48% with either side winning, it's as if World War III has broken out and we all lose. If this occurs, dog-whistling leaders and barking trench commanders remain in power and continue to unleash evil on America.

But perhaps, I misspoke. Maybe World War III doesn't occur from merely a close vote; maybe it's the realization that America is in a second Cold War. If that's the reality then, like our 2016 election, Team Putin becomes the big winner again.

If the vote is inside 55% to 45% with either side winning, the groups still got serious problems.

Once favorable votes outside 55% to 45% occur—and the two out of three tipping point—then the chains of continuous combat are weakened, and evil actors begin to lose followers. The entire group is not singing from the same sheet of music, but they are not vicious combatants either. This is where most good large working groups reside—not great, but not bad.

The national Presidential election is currently scheduled to take place on Tuesday, November 3, 2020. I get it. Our choices suck. No one is excited about choosing between two seventy-five-year-old White guys. Note to self, America. In future elections, we need to give the voters the opportunity to pass the leadership to younger, more diverse candidates.

I'm guessing this upcoming election will be a repeat of the 2016 election, in which most votes were motivated against one of the candidates, not for them. But maybe this time, this flawed strategy can work in our favor. In the upcoming 2020 election, perhaps the Big Risk Doctrine also applies. Are we, as a society, getting too close to Big Risk? Are we getting too close to the chaos, danger, and hate of a divided nation overwhelming us? Is NOW the time to back away from Big Risk? I sure hope two out of three readers of this book— from both tribes—can agree that the answer is unequivocally yes.

I'm sensing we can all agree that it's time to turn. (OK, Son, I'm trying to sneak in only one solution, but we'll need your generation to giddy-up.)

Let's agree on two goals for this election. First, let's turn away from Big Risk. And second, let's get 55% or more of the voters to agree. Remember, the ultimate goal is for two out of three of us to agree so we can become a powerful team once again.

Today's reality is that we are a society badly infected with a mental, mutating virus called Trench Warfare Dementia. And we may have been infected a lot longer than we realize. The first step out of the trenches, or the first round of chemo, is always the toughest to take.

But back to the first goal: turning away from Big Risk. Hmmm … this should be easy. In my entire adult life I have never seen such wildly different candidates running for the same office.

There is no overlap between the way Joe Biden and Donald Trump treat people.

There is no overlap between the way Joe Biden and Donald Trump conduct themselves or their business or their personal values.

There is no overlap between the way Joe Biden and Donald Trump choose to work with our allies around the globe.

And on a personal note, I feel the hate, divisiveness, and evil flowing through our society today have been directly amplified, if not institutionalized, by Donald Trump's constant, dog-whistling rhetoric and tweets. As a White police officer kneeled on a Black man's neck until he took his last breath, we couldn't help but notice the constant stream of inflammatory tweets and outright lies from

President Trump that directly emboldened such heinous and reprehensible acts of violence.

It seems there are clear-cut differences between the two candidates.

Now turning our attention to the second goal: A favorable vote of 55% or above. This election will be a numbers game. It always is. I fear if the vote is inside 52–48, then accusations of voter fraud may keep the results (and our country) locked up in our courts past an inauguration date.

Traditionally, only 60% of eligible voters participate in any given Presidential Election. And with the coronavirus pandemic ravaging our economy and our people, voting will be much more difficult this time around. As a result, each citizen will need to make a determined effort to get out there and vote.

What follows may be seen as inappropriate by many readers, but with the utmost respect and the gentlest kindness, I will now address specific segments of our society.

The Black Community

To the Black community, please do not lose hope in America. Voting results matter. You have seen this ugly story before, and you have endured this dangerous path before. Let's be clear, my tribe has tried every possible legal and illegal way to stifle your vote. I am still somewhat mystified how America could elect a Black man the President of the United States twice but allowed racism to quickly reemerge with a vengeance. But here's the thing—it never left. Racism is a deeply ingrained blight on American culture, one that needs to (finally) be eradicated completely and cut out like a cancer.

To the Black community, please vote. America needs you—now, more than ever—by her side.

My Tribe

To the members of my tribe, who are among my closest friends: What has happened to us?

Look where the alt-right media and hateful, lying, barking trench commanders have taken us. We are not bad, hateful people, but we are clearly cheering for and are being led by some of the most self-righteous, self-centered, brain-dead, and evil idiots in the world! We are not stupid people. We are not fearful people. We are not hateful people. At our very core, we are some of the hardest working and most capable people in America. When I am talking about hard-working American families as the nation's foundation and engine, I am including all of us—my tribe, too. But the reality is that over the past three years, we have become God-like Captains, and we have become dangerous ... to America.

If any member of my tribe still believes that Joe Biden is too liberal to vote for, I am asking them to consider withholding enthusiasm for Trump and simply refraining from voting entirely.

My Wife's Tribe

Ugh ... my house might be a bit chilly the first time my wife reads these comments in print. Ouch!

I get it: you aren't exactly excited about voting for either seventy-five-year-old White guy. You expected a woman at the top of the ticket. You feel betrayed and disappointed, yet again. Life is not fair. Please take some time to reflect and get focused again. Remember

… November is coming. Here's the motivational part. If 100% of my wife's tribe doesn't show up and vote, Donald Trump will probably win, yet again.

My Kid's Tribe

And now for my kid's tribe: The Millennials.

First, let me remind Millennials of our two goals: turn away from Big Risk, and win the Presidential Election by a comfortable margin, so that America will no longer be tied in knots. Again this boils down to a numbers game, but don't worry, I've saved the best for last.

Welcome to adulthood, millennials.

Let me start with my standard disclaimer. I get it. Many of you wanted Bernie. Biden makes you yawn, and most of you think Trump is an asshole. Got it. Life isn't fair. But here's a silver lining: There are about seventy million baby boomers, and now there are around seventy million eligible millennials too, sandwiched in between Generation X, who represent around sixty-five million eligible voters.

For the most part, throughout the writing of this book, I have always presented both sides of the argument and was determined to push us all toward the middle so America could play as a powerful team once again. In the last few chapters, however, I have switched gears, urging us to turn way from Big Risk, NOW! And make no mistake, now, means the Presidential Election this November.

If I read the results of the 2016 election correctly, baby boomers voted in force, but millennials were a bit of a no-show. So what is the reality of these numbers? This dynamic potentially makes millennials America's next Secret Sauce! In November, if America is to turn away from Big Risk and break the chains of a divided nation, we need the millennials to show up at the ballot box and go BOOM!

I have tried my best to change a few votes from the boomers, but the reality is that my generation is getting old and tired and we have been wallowing in self-pity and Trench Warfare Dementia for way too long.

So now it's time to pass the generational baton. Millennials, you have now become America's swing vote! You easily have the size and power to snap America out of its funk by delivering a comfortable victory, signaling a significant course correction for our future performance.

PLEASE. PLEASE. PLEASE. This fall, we need all the millennials and Generation X to vote in November and go Boom!

Fly Safe,

Captain Brad Bartholomew

June 1, 2020

Update, June 9: It's been sickening to watch how President Trump and Attorney General Barr have conducted themselves since the murder of George Floyd. Madeleine Albright thinks it's fascism. My wife thinks it's dystopian. General Mattis thinks it's an assault on our constitution. I think it's plain evil.

And the Black community keeps reminding us, it's just business as usual.

EPILOGUE

I would like to end by explaining what the Lord's Prayer means to me. Again, I fully appreciate and respect the fact that every reader will make their own interpretation of this scripture. Here is the prayer from my New International Version Bible.

Our Father who art in heaven, hallowed be thy name.

Thy kingdom come, thy will be done on earth as it is in heaven.

Give us this day our daily bread.

And forgive us our trespasses,

as we forgive those who trespass against us.

And lead us not into temptation,

but deliver us from evil.

I have taken some liberties with the punctuation and in this version, I use the word "trespasses," while acknowledging that several versions of the Lord's Prayer use the words "debtor" or "sins" instead of "trespasses."

This first two sentences taken together make me wonder if life on earth is the heaven we humans are destined to receive. If so, I am still extremely grateful.

Our Father who art in heaven, hallowed be thy name.

Thy kingdom come, thy will be done on earth as it is in heaven.

The next sentence is the only direct material request. Much of Jesus's ministry involved feeding others. In John 21, Jesus instructs Peter three times to "Feed my sheep and care for them."

Give us this day our daily bread.

The next two sentences, taken together, I think are the downfall of most human beings. We are quick to ask for forgiveness (usually each week at church) and equally quick to point out the faults of others, but most of us are excruciatingly slow to genuinely forgive.

I have a full throttle, Type A personality. I know it's wrong, but for me, *letting go of perceived injustices* is extremely difficult. And letting go happens more often than genuine forgiveness anymore. I'm a slow learner.

And forgive us our trespasses,

as we forgive those who trespass against us.

I've spent much time in self-reflection thinking about those last two sentences.

I think of the next sentence whenever I am clicking on my devices or thinking about buying something I don't really need, or when I flippantly dismiss the consequences of my thoughts, words, or deeds. The entire premise I outline in this book regarding the creation of dysfunctional demands originated from pondering these phrases.

And lead us not into temptation,

When I examine the consequences of our divided society, this final sentence haunts me:

but deliver us from evil.

Thanks for listening,

Brad

WISDOM FROM OTHER AUTHORS

Duckworth, Angela. "Grit—The Power of Passion and Perseverance." Scribner, 2016.

Janis, Irving. "Victims of Groupthink: A Psychological Studies of Foreign-Policy Decisions and Fiascoes." Houghton Mifflin Company, 1972.

Takin, Stan. "Wired for Love—How Understanding Your Partner's Brain and Attachment Style Can Help You Defuse Conflict and Build a Secure Relationship." New Harbinger Publications, Inc., 2011.

Wu, Tim. "The Attention Merchants—The Epic Scramble to Get Inside Our Heads." Vintage Books, 2016.

Gittell, Jody, Hoffer. "The Southwest Airlines Way—Using the Power of Relationships to Achieve High Performance." McGraw-Hill, 2003.

Parker, Jim. "Do the Right Thing—How Dedicated Employees Create Loyal Customers and Large Profits." Pearson Education, Inc., 2008.

Mauldin, John. "Mauldin Economics—Thoughts from the Frontline." A weekly free online economic and investment newsletter - www.mauldineconomics.com

Tepper, Jonathan and Hearn, Denise. "The Myth of Capitalism—Monopolies and the Death of Competition." Wiley, 2019.

Mayer, Jane. "Dark Money—The Hidden History of Billionaires Behind the Rise of the Radical Right." Doubleday, 2016.

Winkler, Adam. "How American Businesses Won Their Civil Rights." Liveright Publishing Corporation, 2018.

McLean, Bethany and Nocera, Joe. "All the Devils Are Here—The Hidden History of the Financial Crisis." Portfolio/Penguin, 2010.

King, Mervyn. "The End of Alchemy: Money, Banking, and the Future of Global Economy." W. W. Norton & Company, 2016.

Albright, Madeleine and Woodward, Bill. "Fascism—A Warning." HarperCollins, 2018.

McChrystal, Stanley. "My Share of the Task," Penguin, 2014.

Olson, Kim. "Iraq and Back—Inside the War to Win the Peace," Naval Institute, 2006.

Morris, Errol, director. "The Fog of War" documentary, 2003.

Mattis, James. "In Union There Is Strength." *Atlantic Magazine* by Jeffery Goldberg, June 3, 2020.

MacLean, Nancy. "Democracy in Chains. The Deep History of the Radical Rights' Stealth Plan for America." Viking, 2017.

Morris, Errol. *The Fog of War*. Sony Classics, 2003.

THANK YOU(S)

First, I must start by giving my greatest appreciation for all of the men and women who kept me safe while flying airplanes. I tried to greet everyone I met with a welcoming smile, but I'm sure there are probably thousands who worked behind the scenes in the aviation industry who I never had opportunity to meet or thank. I hope I contributed as much to the piloting profession as I received, but I specifically need to thank the other three great professions of aviation that work tirelessly to keep airplanes safe: mechanics, air traffic controllers, and dispatchers.

Perhaps I misspoke earlier about our secret sauce. When we pilots, mechanics, air traffic controllers and dispatchers were making a mess of things, at the LUV airline it was our amazing, incredibly hard-working and wonderful flight attendants who toiled on the front lines. Every airline has ugly days—those were the days our professional flight attendants performed miracles.

Next, I need to thank Dr. Sandra Reid, Chair of the Graduate School of Business, Dallas Baptist University. I had the pleasure of her guidance over five years ago when I was contemplating life after flying. During our conversation, I was contemplating graduate school, and inquired about obtaining an advanced degree. After we talked for about an hour, she looked at me and said, "I think you have a book in your head. Why don't you pursue that first?"

I am the author of this book, but I could not have written it without the remarkable expertise of Jennifer Banash, a truly gifted writer and editor. Over forty years ago, I needed to take freshman composition twice to get a passing grade—and apparently, a lifetime spent in the cockpit has failed to substantially improve my writing skills. Jennifer's contribution to bringing this book to fruition is immeasurable.

And last, but certainly not least, without the love and support of my wife, Beth, nothing I (we) have ever accomplished would be meaningful.